ISRAEL'S MISSION

DISCOVERY GUIDE

That the World May Know® with Ray Vander Laan

ISRAEL'S MISSION

─── 5 LESSONS ON ───

**Becoming a Kingdom of Priests
in a Prodigal World**

DISCOVERY GUIDE

**EXPERIENCE THE BIBLE IN
HISTORICAL CONTEXT**
Ray Vander Laan
with Stephen and Amanda Sorenson

ZONDERVAN

Israel's Mission Discovery Guide
Copyright © 2015 by Ray Vander Laan

This title is also available as a Zondervan ebook. Visit www.zondervan.com/ebooks.

Requests for information should be addressed to:
Zondervan, 3900 *Sparks Dr. SE, Grand Rapids, Michigan 49546*

Focus on the Family and the accompanying logo and design are federally registered trademarks of Focus on the Family, 8605 *Explorer Drive, Colorado Springs, Colorado 80920.*

That the World May Know is a trademark of Focus on the Family.

ISBN 978-0-310-81061-2

All maps created by International Mapping.

All photos are courtesy of Ray Vander Laan, Paul Murphy, and Grooters Productions.

All Scripture quotations, unless otherwise indicated, are taken from The Holy Bible, *New International Version*®, *NIV*®. Copyright © 1973, 1978, 1984, 2011 by Biblica, Inc.® Used by permission. All rights reserved worldwide.

Scripture quotations marked ESV are taken from *The Holy Bible, English Standard Version,* copyright © 2001 by Crossway Bibles, a division of Good News Publishers. Used by permission. All rights reserved.

Scripture quotations marked KVJ are taken from the King James Version of the Bible.

Any Internet addresses (websites, blogs, etc.) and telephone numbers in this book are offered as a resource. They are not intended in any way to be or imply an endorsement by Zondervan, nor does Zondervan vouch for the content of these sites and numbers for the life of this book.

*Cover design: Do**More**Good®*
Cover photography: Grooters Productions
Interior design: Ben Fetterley, Denise Froehlich

First Printing April 2015 / Printed in the United States of America

CONTENTS

INTRODUCTION

The Bible makes it clear that the one true God desires to be known by all people.

The Hebrew word for "know," *yadah*, means more than rational awareness of facts. It implies intimate personal experience. For example, a literal translation of Genesis 4:1 says, "Now Adam knew [*yadah*] Eve his wife, and she conceived and bore Cain" (ESV). Thus "knowing God" is not only knowing about him theologically but also experiencing a relationship with him. As people experience him, they will acknowledge him as the one true God and give him the praise he alone deserves.

The Lord makes himself known by what he says and does. As he acts in history, people experience him, come to *yadah* him, and develop a relationship with him. The deliverance of his people from slavery in Egypt, for example, reveals God's intention that the Hebrews, the Egyptians, and even Pharaoh would know him as they experienced his power and greatness.[1] This thread runs through all of Scripture: The creation must know its Creator; the nations, their King; and all people, their Savior.

In the opening chapters of the Bible, God entrusted Adam and Eve with a mission to fill the earth, use it wisely, and rule it well.[2] This mission of caring for God's creation was disrupted when Adam and Eve sinned, but God did not give up on using the humans he created as his partners. Beginning with Abraham (the first Hebrew) and continuing through his descendants, God chose a people to be his partners in blessing and restoring his creation.[3] He gave Israel the mission of being a kingdom of priests for the nations[4] that would make him known so that all people would experience him. Although it is God's redeeming grace that restores alienated people to God, he entrusted to his people the mission of making himself known.

The central message of the gospel is that God sent his Son, Jesus, to redeem people who were alienated from him because of their sin. Jesus' atoning death and resurrection are the source of eternal life and the only way to be restored to relationship with the Creator. But we must not overlook the way Jesus also carried out the mission of making God known so that all people could be restored to relationship with his Father. Just as God called Israel to be the light of the world and to make God's name known, Jesus did the same. By his words and actions Jesus revealed God's nature, making it possible for people to *know* him.

The mission of making God known to all people was not completed during Jesus' ministry on earth. Jesus entrusted it to his disciples during his last teaching before ascending to heaven. Matthew records his words, sometimes called "the Great Commission," most succinctly:

> *Then Jesus came to them and said, "All authority in heaven and on earth has been given to me. Therefore go and make disciples of all nations, baptizing them in the name of the Father and of the Son and of the Holy Spirit, and teaching them to obey everything I have commanded you. And surely I am with you always, to the very end of the age."*

> **Matthew 28:18–20**

By this commission, Jesus' disciples became the light of the world, people who would live in such a way as to hallow God's name — make his character and reputation known to the nations.[5] Those who followed Jesus were to be a royal priesthood that put God on display by their actions and words.[6]

Christians have always believed that this mission is the task of the community of God's people. To be a follower of Jesus is to become part of a journey that spans millennia as it moves toward its final destination — the restoration of all things! It is to participate in the greatest undertaking ever known. It is to join Abraham, Sarah, Moses, Ruth, David, Elijah, Isaiah, Mary, Peter, and Paul in partnership with the Creator of the universe as his instruments, bearing the good news of redemption to all people. That is the clear meaning of Jesus' words.

Sometimes, however, Christians have limited this mission to "evangelism" or sharing the message that God's only Son has come and offers salvation in his name. Certainly that gospel, or "good news," is at the heart of the mission God has given us. But the mission God has entrusted to his people does not originate from Matthew 28 alone; it comes from the entire Bible. The mission God has given to his people is the thread that ties all of Scripture together from the beginning of time until all things are completed.

The mission continues in God's people today. Although the increasingly secular state of Western culture is sobering, leading some Christians to voice resignation to the inevitable decline of a broken world, God's desire for all people to know him has not diminished. Never has there been a greater opportunity to serve as God's coworkers, his kingdom of priests, who mediate his presence and make him *known*. We must not only declare the good news of his saving work but also live as concrete examples of *knowing* God by displaying his character through our actions.

The Text in Its Context

Throughout human history, God has spoken and acted in the context of the cultures in which his people lived. Abraham cut up animals to seal a blood covenant much as the Hittites did. The design of the temple of the Lord built by Solomon in Jerusalem was familiar to the neighboring cultures of God's people. In Corinth where clay and marble body parts were displayed as votive offerings to the pagan god of healing, Paul describes the community of faith as a body made up of many parts. God had a unique purpose for communicating his message through these culturally familiar concepts and practices that made the point of his message strikingly clear and relevant. Thus the cultural setting in which God placed his revelation is useful for understanding the message and application of Scripture, much like the study of the language of the ancient culture provides for the interpreter.[7]

Understanding the message of Scripture involves more than knowing what words mean. The circumstances and conditions of the people of the Bible are unique to their times. We most clearly understand God's truth when we know the cultural context within which he spoke and acted and the perspective of the people with whom he communicated. So we must enter the world of the Bible and familiarize ourselves with its culture. By learning how to think and approach life as Abraham, Moses, Ruth, John the Baptist, and Paul did, modern Christians will deepen their appreciation of God's Word.

Unfortunately, many Christians do not have even a basic knowledge of the world and people of the Bible. To address that problem, we will be studying the people and events of the Bible in their geographical, historical, and cultural contexts. Once we know the who, what, and where of a Bible story, we will be able to understand the why. By deepening our understanding of God's Word, we begin to experience God and grow in our relationship with him.

The people to whom God revealed himself in the Scriptures lived in the ancient Middle East where people typically described their world and themselves in concrete terms. Their language was one of pictures, metaphors, and examples rather than ideas, definitions, and abstractions. Whereas we might describe God as omniscient or omnipresent (knowing everything and present everywhere), they would describe God by saying, "The Lord is my Shepherd." Thus, the Bible is filled with concrete images: God is our Father, and we are his children. God is the Potter, and we are the clay. Jesus is the Lamb killed on Passover. The kingdom of heaven is like the yeast a woman took and mixed into flour. He will separate the people as a shepherd separates the sheep from the goats.

In that world, the best way to know God is to observe him in action rather than attempt to define him with doctrine. His great redemptive acts are remembered and retold because God is known by what he does. Faith as action is preferred over faith as a rational concept, so understanding the walk God desires is not simply memorizing laws, rules, and regulations but remembering how we — always *we* — lived in the past both obediently and disobediently. In this context, the ancient stories are more than simply history. They define our faith — the God we serve and the walk he desires. Therefore, we join their story rather than simply knowing their story. We were slaves in Egypt. We heard God at Sinai. We journeyed through the desert. We worshipped idols. We repented and were restored.

In addition, Eastern thought emphasizes the *process* of learning as much or more than the end result. Whereas Westerners tend to collect information to find the right answer, Hebrew thought stresses the process of discovery as well as learning how to find right answers. So as you go through this study, use it as an opportunity to deepen your understanding of who God is and to grow in your relationship with him.

The record of God's reclaiming and restoring his broken world is called the Bible, Scripture, or "the Text" in this study. Having studied in the Jewish world, I believe it is important to communicate clearly how the nature of that inspired book is understood. It can be misleading to speak of Old and New Testaments. While there are helpful elements in these descriptions, they can be interpreted to mean old and outdated and the new replacement. Nothing, in my opinion, is further from the truth. Yes, the "New Testament" describes the great advance of God's plan with the arrival of the Messiah and the promise of his continued and completed work.[8] The Old lays the foundational events and people God used to advance his work. But the Bible is not complete without both Testaments. It is one Bible, one plan to reclaim God's world, one way to restore *shalom*. To focus on that unity, I will at times refer to the "Hebrew Text" (Old Testament) and the "Christian Text" (New Testament) — together the inspired, infallible Word of God.

The Land

This study was filmed in several locations in Israel and Jordan. However, these are modern political designations and will be referred to by their biblical names in the study itself. Several terms are used to identify the land God promised to Abraham. The Hebrew Text refers to it as Canaan or Israel. The Christian Text calls it Judea. After the Second Jewish Revolt (AD 132 – 135), it was known as Palestine. Each of these names resulted from historical events taking place in the land at the time they were coined.

Canaan is one of the earliest designations of the Promised Land. The word probably meant "purple," referring to the dye used to color garments worn by royalty, a dye produced from murex shell-fish found along the coast of Phoenicia. The word for the color eventually was used to refer to the people who produced the dye and purple cloth for trade. Hence, in the Bible, Canaanite refers to a "trader" or "merchant" (Zechariah 14:21), as well as to a person from the "land of purple," or Canaan. Originally the word applied only to the coast of Phoenicia; later it applied to the whole region.

Israel, the Old Testament designation for the Promised Land, derives from the patriarch Jacob, whom God renamed Israel (Genesis 32:28). His descendants were known as the children of Israel. After the Israelites conquered Canaan in the time of Joshua, the name of the people became the designation for the land itself (in the same way it had with the Canaanites). When the nation split following the death of Solomon, the name Israel was applied to the northern kingdom and its territory, while the southern land was called Judah. After the fall of the northern kingdom to the Assyrians in 722 BC, the entire land was again called Israel.

The word *Palestine* comes from the people of the coastal plain, the Philistines. The Egyptians used Palestine long before the Roman period to refer to the land where the Philistines lived — Philistia — but the Roman emperor Hadrian popularized the term as part of his campaign to eliminate Jewish influence from the area (about one hundred years after Jesus' death). During New Testament times, the Promised Land was called Judea (which means "Jewish"), which technically referred to the land that had been the nation of Judah. The Romans divided the land into several provinces, including Judea, Samaria, and Galilee (the three main divisions during Jesus' time); Gaulanitis, the Decapolis, and Perea (east of the Jordan River); and Idumaea (Edom) and Nabatea (in the south). These further divisions add to the rich historical and cultural background God prepared for the coming of Jesus and the beginning of his church.

Today the names *Israel* and *Palestine* are often used to designate the land God gave to Abraham. Both terms are politically charged. *Palestine* is used by the Arabs living in the central part of the country, while *Israel* is used by the Jews to indicate the modern political

State of Israel. In this study *Israel* is used in the biblical sense. This choice does not indicate a political statement regarding the current struggle in the Middle East, but is chosen to best reflect the biblical designation for the land.

God Reclaims His World

From the beginning, God's plan was to reclaim his world that had been broken by sin and to use people as his partners in that effort. He chose a people, Israel, and a place — the Promised Land at the crossroads of the ancient world — to make his name known. The nations of the ancient world traveled the Via Maris, the major trade route that stretched from Egypt to Babylon and ran through Israel. By living in the Promised Land and obeying God's commandments, his chosen people couldn't help but display his character and make him known to the entire world.

Yet they struggled to be faithful. They were blessed by God's hand but repeatedly turned away to worship the gods of the nations around them. Again and again, God's prophets called them back to him, back to their mission: " 'I, even I, am the LORD, and apart from me there is no savior. I have revealed and saved and proclaimed — I, and not some foreign god among you. You are my witnesses,' declares the LORD, 'that I am God' " (Isaiah 43:11 - 12).

Eventually God allowed pagan nations to conquer the land and carry his people away to foreign lands. The Assyrian dispersion and the Babylonian exile spread God-fearing Jewish people around the known world. Many of them renewed their faithfulness to God, even returning to Jerusalem to celebrate the yearly feasts that God had commanded. God was preparing his people and the world for the next stage in his great plan of salvation. His people would need to learn to live *so that the world may know* — the entire world, not just one small place — that he is God.

The arena had changed, but the mission had not. The people of God would reveal him to others in places like Rome, Athens, and the cities of Roman provinces like Syria and Macedonia. The most pagan of all provinces, Asia, would become a stronghold for the followers of

God and the Messiah Jesus. They would serve him while the nations of the world watched and listened. Our mission as God's people today is the same one God gave to the Israelites, the same one Jesus gave to his disciples. We are to live obediently *within* the world so that through us, *it may know that our God is the one true God.*

God's partners have always struggled to carry out this task faithfully. A Jewish rabbi describes the options as assimilating, separating, or engaging the culture to which we seek to make God known. Noah separated and had little influence on the world around him.[9] Lot assimilated and became much like the oppressive people of the city in which he lived.[10] Abraham lived a righteous life and was known as a "prince of God" by his neighbors.[11] And Western Christianity tends to separate our walk with God from our responsibility to the world in which he has placed us.

My hope is that many of us will seek to engage our culture and be a blessing wherever God places us.

God wants his people in the game, not on the bench. We do not have to be powerful or a majority to fulfill our task. Christianity, like Judaism, had its finest hours when it was a poor and weak minority that was faithful to carrying out God's mission in a broken world.[12] I pray that seeing the Bible in the context in which God placed its stories and characters helps you to understand how to respond to his revelation with greater passion for faithfulness. I pray that God's mission for you becomes ever more compelling. We are the witnesses — the royal priesthood — through whom spiritually lost people come to know the God of the universe who loves them and longs to restore them.

ABRAHAM AND SARAH AND THREE STRANGERS

The Bible opens with the story of God bringing order out of watery chaos. His amazing creative work accomplished, God entrusted it to the care of our human ancestors, Adam and Eve. He gave them the responsibility to care for it and the freedom to choose how to rule and manage it. From that point on, the biblical story reveals a series of disappointing choices made by God's human partners that resulted in the return of chaos to God's created order.

Adam and Eve chose to eat from the one tree God had forbidden. Their oldest son, Cain, murdered his brother, Abel. With each passing generation, humankind became increasingly corrupt and wicked. By the time Noah entered the story, the heart of God was deeply troubled because "every inclination of the thoughts of the human heart was only evil all the time" (Genesis 6:5). In order to end the evil, God wiped the human race from the face of the earth, sparing only the family of Noah because he was a righteous man who walked with God. But even the cleansing of the Great Flood didn't change things for long. Noah's grandchildren refused to "fill the earth" as God had instructed, preferring to settle together and make a name for themselves by building a city with a great tower — as if to challenge God himself (Genesis 9:1 – 11:8).

Surprisingly, God did not give up on his human partners! After generations of silence, the story picks up again with Terah, Abraham's father, leaving Ur of the Chaldeans (believed to be near the city of Mosul in northern Iraq) to move his family to Canaan. They did not complete the journey, but settled in Harran, a few miles north of today's Turkish/Syrian border (Genesis 11:27 – 32). After Terah died, God commanded Abraham to leave his present life — land, community, and even family — and "go to the land I will show you." The offer came with the promise of great blessing — a message of hope and mission not just for Abraham, but for him to be a conduit of God's blessing to all people on earth (Genesis 12:1 – 3).

God was asking Abraham to turn his back on the life he had known and to become his partner in redeeming a world in chaos! In a dramatic reversal of the choices many earlier characters in the biblical story made, Abraham committed himself to do what was right and just in the eyes of the Lord. Responding in faith, he left Harran. From that point on, Abraham would be different; he walked God's path and taught his children to do the same:

> *Then the* Lord *said … "For I have chosen him, so that he will direct his children and his household after him to keep the way of the* Lord *by doing what is right and just, so that the* Lord *will bring about for Abraham what he has promised him."*

Genesis 18:17, 19

Whereas Adam and Eve failed to faithfully obey God, Abraham eagerly demonstrated what a faithful partnership with God looks like. By choosing to be God's partner in restoring *shalom* to a world in chaos and bringing alienated sinners back into relationship with God, Abraham became a model for all who have come after him. The Jewish writer, Matthew, certainly intended to communicate more than just biological descent when he began Jesus' family tree with Abraham. Although Abraham could never effect the changes in a sinful world that the Messiah did, this Bedouin nomad lived in a way that showed how the world could be when God's people live according to his design. Since everyone who places his or her faith in Jesus is in effect a child of Abraham (Galatians 3:7 – 9), let's discover more about this faithful partner who lived to be a blessing to everyone he met.

Opening Thoughts (3 minutes)

The Very Words of God

> The LORD had said to Abram, "Go from your country, your people and your father's household to the land I will show you.
> "I will make you into a great nation, and I will bless you; I will make your name great, and you will be a blessing. I will bless those who bless you, and whoever curses you I will curse; and all peoples on earth will be blessed through you."
>
> *Genesis 12:1 – 3*

Think About It

In the Bible story, the Lord is portrayed as the One who *redeems* his people and calls them to be his "partners" in redeeming others. In Western Christianity, we tend to think of redemption as being synonymous with salvation. While there is no doubt that the reality of God's salvation is included in what it means to *redeem*, the word actually has a broader meaning in the context of the Bible.

Talk for a moment about what is involved in redeeming something or someone. What examples of redemption can you think of (in history, contemporary life, or the Bible)? What does the act of redeeming indicate about the value of what is redeemed? Who redeems, and why? What is the response to and result of redemption? What insight do these observations give you into the broader meaning of *redeem*?

DVD Notes (31 minutes)

Partners in making God known

Life in an ancient city

The patriarch's role and responsibilities
Go'el—"to redeem"

Beth ab—"the father's house"

Using the resources of the Father's house
Abraham

Boaz

Hosea

Jesus

Redeem with everything you've got!

DVD Discussion (8 minutes)

1. In what ways does what you learned about Arad and the lifestyle of people who lived there help you to better understand the world of Abraham? What particularly impressed you?

FACT FILE: ANCIENT ARAD

This study was filmed at Tel Arad in the Negev Wilderness. Although few people visit this fascinating archaeological site, it has been extensively excavated and provides insight into the lives of people who inhabited this area throughout the time of the Hebrew Bible.

- Founded before 3000 BC as a trading center, Arad is located at the edge of the desert between the land of the shepherds and the arable land to the north. Here, farmers brought their flour and olive oil to trade for the shepherd's wool and cheese. During later times, it served as a military fortress.
- In Abraham's time, Arad covered twenty-five acres and had an estimated population of two to three thousand.
- The king of Arad attacked the Israelites in the desert before they entered the Promised Land. He was eventually defeated by Joshua (Numbers 21:1 – 4; 33:40; Joshua 12:14) and the city was given to the Kenites, the family of Moses' father-in-law, Jethro (Judges 1:16 – 17).
- The upper part of Arad was a fortress the kings of Judah built to control the border between Israel and Edom. Solomon built the first fortress, which the Egyptians destroyed and Jehoshaphat rebuilt. Around 567 BC, Nebuchadnezzar of Babylon destroyed Arad. Nearly two hundred potsherds with writing on them (*ostraca*) have been found in excavations of the Israelite fortress of Arad. These ostraca are significant because they illustrate three hundred years of Hebrew language usage.

**FORTRESS OF ARAD AS BUILT BY SOLOMON AND
DESTROYED BY THE BABYLONIANS AROUND 567 BC**

**THE CITY OF ARAD, WHICH EXISTED
AT THE TIME OF ABRAHAM**

- In their fortress, the Israelites built a temple comprised of a large courtyard, a Holy Place, and a Holy of Holies. Bowls found in the ruins have inscriptions probably meaning, "set apart for the priest." Archaeologists believe Hezekiah (eighth century BC) destroyed this temple during his reform of the religious system and filled in its courtyard so the temple could not be used.

- The temple is a wonderful reminder that God's people have been serving him for nearly four millennia and continue to "partner" with him in his plan of redemption. Although often unfaithful, his followers have not been failures. God used their service in his plan just as he continues to use his followers today. May we be found faithful to continue the mission.

2. What has been your impression of a patriarchal society, and in what ways do the cornerstones of the ancient Hebrew patriarchal society — *go'el*, meaning to "redeem," and *beth ab*, meaning "the father's house" — differ from what has been your understanding?

3. Throughout human history, God has always sought to redeem and restore his lost children to his house. We sometimes think of the lost as pagans and sinners who need to be saved. Although that is true, redemption is bigger than that. How does our attitude and motivation toward those who are lost change when we see them as God does — as his very own children — children who are in great trouble, overwhelmed by debt they can never pay, lost and cannot find their way home?

FOR GREATER UNDERSTANDING
A Land I Will Show You ...

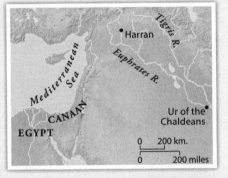

When he was seventy-five years old, Abraham obeyed God's command and set out from Harran with his family and possessions to go to "the land I will show you" (Genesis 12:1). The land was Canaan.

A wealthy shepherd, Abraham lived primarily in or near the Negev desert where nomadic shepherds graze their flocks today. He also wandered into the Judah Mountains, possibly to graze his sheep in the harvested fields during the summer and fall—a practice that still exists.

After Abraham and Lot parted company, Abraham walked through the entire land of Canaan to see the extent of God's promise to him and his descendants (Genesis 13:14–18). He returned to Hebron, where he lived when the three strangers came to visit.

4. At Mount Sinai, God gave the Hebrew people a mission: to be a kingdom of priests who would extend God's reign by obeying his commands and putting him on display so that all people and nations would be drawn to him. Hundreds of years earlier, the Hebrews' ancestors, Abraham and Sarah, were already living out that mission. They provided for the Hebrews — as well as for us — a powerful example of how to be God's partners in redeeming and restoring his lost children.

    a. In what ways does Abraham and Sarah's response to their three visitors reveal the depth of their commitment to live out that mission in their world?

    b. What might a similar commitment to restoring the lost to God's *beth ab* look like in our world?

Small Group Bible Discovery and Discussion (13 minutes)

Extending the Blessing of the Beth Ab

Life in the ancient Middle East centered around the extended family or household, which was called the "father's house" or *beth ab* in Hebrew. Such a family could comprise thirty, fifty, or more people representing several generations: the head of the family (known as the patriarch), his wife or wives, his younger brothers, unmarried children, and married sons with their families (a woman customarily joined the *beth ab* of her husband). The patriarch controlled all family resources, using them to protect and care for each family member.

In this setting, the *beth ab* was the context through which each member was connected to the rest of society. If a member lost connection to the family due to oppression, capture by enemies, poverty, or bad choices, the patriarch was responsible to restore the "marginalized" member to the family. Anyone who found himself or herself without a *beth ab* was in serious trouble. Widows and orphans were particularly vulnerable because they had no means of support or protection outside the *beth ab*.

1. Abraham was a patriarch with a mission. He recognized his role as God's partner in extending the Father's house to bless all people and nations and to put God on display in such a way as to attract those who were estranged from him, so that they could experience restoration to the *beth ab*. Let's see how Abraham (and Sarah) modeled this mission when three total strangers suddenly appeared at his desert home. Read Genesis 18:2 - 8.

    a. What do we learn about Abraham's servant heart? (See Genesis 18:2 - 5.)

    b. What evidence do we see that Abraham taught his family about caring for people in need — the poor, the oppressed, the alien — according to God's desire? (See Genesis 18:6, 19; 19:1 - 3. Note: As Abraham's nephew, Lot had previously lived in Abraham's *beth ab*.)

    c. What indicates that Abraham spared no expense in serving his three guests? (See Genesis 18:6 - 8.)

POINT TO PONDER
Beyond Hospitality

Even a quick reading of the story of Abraham, Sarah, and the three strangers reveals the couple's commitment to serve others with all their resources. But there's more to the story than first meets the eye.

Older men in the Middle East don't run. To do so is considered shameful. Even more remarkable, this story takes place in the desert during the heat of the day, and Abraham recently had been circumcised (Genesis 17:26–27). Yet he, like the father of the Prodigal Son (whom we will study in a future session), ran to greet these strangers. He willingly endured shame and significant discomfort to reach out to the strangers who crossed his path.

Abraham didn't just serve his guests the leftovers. He selected a choice, tender "calf," not necessarily the offspring of a cow, but a young animal that was a rare delicacy — the highest sign of hospitality in the world of desert nomads. He had Sarah prepare a huge amount of the finest fresh bread. This was not the everyday barley flour bread; it was made of the very best wheat flour. The amount Sarah made could have fed more than a hundred people, not just three! To top it off, they also offered curds (like yogurt) and milk, which is highly esteemed in the desert culture and served as a symbol of high honor.

In every way, at significant expense, Abraham and Sarah communicated concern for their visitors. They displayed the Father's house to the best of their ability. No wonder their response became the model for compassionate treatment of those in need for all of God's people to this day.

2. Matthew began his gospel by identifying Jesus as a descendant of Abraham (see Matthew 1:1 – 17). With what mandate does Matthew end his gospel, and what earlier command and promise does it echo (see Genesis 12:1 – 3; Matthew 28:19 – 20)?

    a.   According to Paul, what connection do believers have to Abraham through Jesus? (See Galatians 3:14, 29.)

    b.   What, then, is the mission of God's people today?

3.   When Jesus taught about the kingdom of heaven in Matthew 13:33 and mentioned the large amount of flour made into bread, what story would the Jewish people — who knew their Scriptures very well — have likely remembered? What picture would it have given them about the kingdom of heaven, the Father's house?

DID YOU KNOW?
Teaching about the Kingdom of Heaven

Jesus often taught about the kingdom of heaven. In the context of Jewish thought, the kingdom of heaven appears in any situation — here and in the life to come — in which God's will is done. First-century Jewish people referred to heaven as a way to avoid saying and possibly misusing the sacred name of God.

Through the Matthew 13:33 parable, Jesus compared this kingdom with yeast. Immediately his audience connected with the daily process of baking bread and the practice of saving a bit of leavened dough to use as yeast for the next day's bread. The obvious point is the inevitable spread of God's coming reign. Like yeast, one cannot see how it works, yet it slowly spreads and affects the entire batch. As God's people accept Jesus as Savior and do his will as Lord, his reign will expand.

Because the Jews of Jesus' day were well-versed in the Text, it also was possible for a teacher to allude to a Scripture passage simply by using a key word, phrase, or image from an ancient story. The teacher knew the audience would recognize the reference and understand that the content of the earlier story was part of the present teaching. So when Jesus told the parable of the woman mixing yeast with a large amount of flour, his audience no doubt recognized its connection to the story of the Lord and two angels visiting Abraham and Sarah.

Not only did Jesus indicate that the kingdom of heaven spreads like yeast, he hinted that the nature of this kingdom is similar to the compassionate, concerned actions of Abraham and Sarah for the three strangers in need! They model for us how to display the loving protection and care of the *beth ab* to those who are marginalized and thereby become God's partners in redeeming his lost children.

Faith Lesson (4 minutes)

The mission that the God of the universe entrusts to his people — to display his character by demonstrating compassion for those in need — began in ancient times in the Negev desert with Abraham and Sarah. It continued throughout biblical history with significant moments in which God's people acted similarly and brought lost children back into the "Father's house." We have been given a truly amazing privilege and responsibility to share through our actions and words the message of redemption that God offers to everyone in our broken world.

I want to share with you an image that conveys a sense of the opportunity we have. It occurred during the filming of this session. In the tent of a Bedouin family, the family patriarch offered us fresh camel's milk. One could sense from his wife and eight children the honor we were being given. Neither our host nor his family drank but simply sat and watched in silence as they honored us with this symbol of great hospitality. We were of a different culture, race, nationality, and religion. They honored us anyway. It is hard to describe the overwhelming sense of appreciation we felt. It was as if God gave us a lesson in how we are to present ourselves and hence our God to those among us (or strangers who enter our lives) who are in need.

1. Jesus said to his disciples, "You are the light of the world. A town built on a hill cannot be hidden. Neither do people light a lamp and put it under a bowl. Instead they put it on its stand, and it gives light to everyone in the house. In the same way, let your light shine before others, that they may see your good deeds and glorify your Father in heaven" (Matthew 5:14 - 16).

    a. What impact might those of us who claim to follow Jesus have on our increasingly secular culture if we imitate Abraham and Jesus — and display God and his ways by being a blessing to other people, whether they be friends or even enemies, strangers or well-known public figures?

    b. As you think about your daily life, what opportunities do you have to put God on display — to be the light on a hill — and invite people to be redeemed and to experience the blessings of the Father's house?

2. Who are the marginalized people you see who live outside the family of God, and what blessings do they need that God has given you to share with them?

   a. How eager are you to share God's blessing with them, and how much are you willing to sacrifice to do so?

Closing (1 minute)

Read Genesis 12:2–3 aloud together: "I will make you into a great nation, and I will bless you; I will make your name great, and you will be a blessing. I will bless those who bless you, and whoever curses you I will curse; and all peoples on earth will be blessed through you."

Then pray, thanking God for the blessing of his *beth ab,* praising him for the miracle of his redemption that restores even the most broken, lost, and hopeless children to his faithful care. Thank God for the privilege of being a blessing to his lost children. Ask him to give you a willing heart, generous spirit, compassionate wisdom, and mighty strength as you seek to display to a watching world the God who redeems.

Memorize

I will make you into a great nation, and I will bless you; I will make your name great, and you will be a blessing. I will bless those who bless you, and whoever curses you I will curse; and all peoples on earth will be blessed through you.

Genesis 12:2–3

Restoring the Lost to the Father's House

In-Depth Personal Study Sessions

Day One | Partners in God's Redemptive Plan

The Very Words of God

> *But you are a chosen people, a royal priesthood, a holy nation, God's special possession, that you may declare the praises of him who called you out of darkness into his wonderful light. Once you were not a people, but now you are the people of God; once you had not received mercy, but now you have received mercy.*
>
> *1 Peter 2:9 – 10*

Bible Discovery

Understanding the Big Picture of Redemption

Christians commonly think of God's message of redemption in the Bible in terms of the well-known words: "For God so loved the world that he gave his one and only Son, that whoever believes in him shall not perish but have eternal life" (John 3:16). Although these words are an excellent summary of the gospel message, it is limiting to view God's redemptive work on our behalf as solely deliverance from sin's bondage, or salvation. Such a view is biblical, but in the words of Christopher Wright, "it is not biblical enough."[1] Redemption in God's framework encompasses salvation — *deliverance from* — and more than that, it is *restoration to.*

The Text frequently uses redeem (Hebrew, *ga'al*) to describe God's actions as our Redeemer (Hebrew, *go'el*). God's plan for restoring *shalom* to his broken world includes rescuing alienated sinners *and* bringing them back into relationship with him, as well as restoring relationships with others and even with the creation itself. Restoring *shalom* is a mission in which God has given his people a vital role.

1. What understanding do you gain about the big picture of God's redemption from the following verses?

God's Plan of Redemption	Israel's Deliverance from Slavery	Jesus' Redemptive Work for All Humanity
Bondage or circumstance from which a family member needs to be freed	Exodus 3:8; 6:6	John 8:34–36; Romans 6:16–18
The redeemer's action to secure redemption	Deuteronomy 7:8	Galatians 4:4–5
The effort or cost to set the marginalized person free	Exodus 6:6	1 Corinthians 6:19–20; Mark 10:45
Full restoration to the community	1 Chronicles 17:21–22	Colossians 1:13–14

2. God acted to restore his lost children fully so that they would believe in him as the one true God, come to know him as their Redeemer, and in response serve him in faithful obedience and worship. What do the following verses reveal about God's full redemption of Israel, which involved political, economic, social, and spiritual deliverance and restoration?

   a. Political (Exodus 1:8 – 14)

   b. Economic (Exodus 3:8; 12:35 – 36; Deuteronomy 26:15)

c. Social (Exodus 2:1 – 2; 20:13 – 17)

d. Spiritual (Exodus 4:22 – 23; 25:8 – 9; 40:34 – 35)

3. Why did Jesus come to earth, die, and rise again — which
   resulted in people believing in him, trusting in him, and
   committing themselves to walk in the way of the Lord? (See
   Luke 1:68; Galatians 3:14.)

DID YOU REALIZE?

In Israel's world, *redeem* was in fact a secular, not religious, concept. It
was derived from a tribal culture's social practices. The family, especially
the patriarch, was responsible for the well-being of all who belonged to the
clan and for providing hospitality to the stranger. If anyone was marginalized
from the kin group, every effort was to be made to restore that person to
the community.

Not only did God desire freedom for his people, he wanted to reclaim them
as his family members who knew him intimately and served him faithfully.
When they were freed from slavery in Egypt, God instructed them to build a
tent — *mishkan* (tabernacle) — and outlined the sacrificial practices through
which he would provide forgiveness and restoration — redemption — to his
household!

Reflection

God's redemption of his people involves restoration at all levels. Although spiritual restoration, or *salvation* as it is often labeled, is the foundation of his redemption, God acts to restore his lost children fully. He not only set the Hebrews free from slavery in Egypt, he provided the opportunity for them to live as a forgiven and godly community that would experience and display his blessing for all the world to see. They were redeemed, and God was their Redeemer.

Jesus' message of redemption echoes the redemption of Israel. The salvation he offers sets us free from slavery to sin. As his followers, we are to become a blessed community of people who serve and worship our Redeemer and display his character and blessing to the world as we love and care for those who are marginalized.

Psalm 103:2 – 6 is an offering of praise for the fullness of God's redemption:

> *Praise the L*ORD*, my soul, and forget not all his benefits — who forgives all your sins and heals all your diseases, who redeems your life from the pit and crowns you with love and compassion, who satisfies your desires with good things so that your youth is renewed like the eagle's. The L*ORD *works righteousness and justice for all the oppressed.*

The many dimensions of God's redemption provide not only freedom from bondage to sin but the blessing of deliverance from the effects of sin in general. Take some time to read the following passages from the Text — both the Old and New Testaments — and seek to comprehend what God's restoration of *beth ab* looks like. Think about how God wants his kingdom to be put on display so that his lost, marginalized children choose to experience his redemption.

The Text	Imagine God's will being done on earth so that:
Ex. 22:22–24	
Lev. 19:18	
Deut. 10:19	
Deut. 14:28–29	
Deut. 15:7–8	
Ps. 68:5	
Isa. 58:6–7	
Matt. 19:21	
Luke 14:13–14	
Heb. 13:2–3	
James 1:27	

Then remember, Jesus Christ "gave himself for us to redeem us from all wickedness and to purify for himself a people that are his very own, eager to do what is good" (Titus 2:14). May his grace be with you as you seek to do what is right and share his blessing with others.

Memorize

> *Praise be to the Lord, the God of Israel, because he has come to his people and redeemed them.*
>
> *Luke 1:68*

Day Two | Outside the Father's House

The Very Words of God

> *But Ruth replied, "Don't urge me to leave you or to turn back from you. Where you go I will go, and where you stay I will stay. Your people will be my people and your God my God. Where you die I will die, and there I will be buried. May the LORD deal with me, be it ever so severely, if even death separates you and me."*
>
> *Ruth 1:16 – 17*

Bible Discovery

Ruth and Naomi: Two Widows Face Insurmountable Difficulties

The story of Ruth, Naomi, and Boaz is one of the most moving accounts in the Bible. The events occurred during the period of the judges, about a century before David became king of Israel. Set in the midst of great hardship and tragic loss, the story focuses on loyalty and faithfulness in stark contrast to the pagan Moabite culture from which Ruth originated, and the frequent unfaithfulness of God's people during that time. The story is also a clear example of God's faithfulness in bringing about his plan of redemption using unexpected partners in amazing ways.

The book of Ruth begins with an Israelite family — Elimelek, his wife Naomi, and their two sons, Mahlon and Kilion — living in Moab. Originally from Bethlehem of Judah, the family left the land of its inheritance because of a famine. Tragedy soon struck. Elimelek died. Both of Naomi's sons married Moabite women, and within ten years the sons died also, leaving Naomi and her daughters-in-law outside the kin group of her husband.

It is hard for us as modern readers to comprehend the hopeless situation in which the three women found themselves. They lacked not only the intimacy of a family group, which is a tragic situation in any time and place, but were outside the father's house — cut off from its protection and provision. Their losses were devastating in every way. They were a non-family with no means of providing for themselves. Options for such marginalized women were few and unpleasant. Completely dependent on the generosity of others, they faced starvation or worse.

1. Please begin this study by reading the entire book of Ruth. Then consider how these widows responded to their desperate situation.

    a. What one piece of good news did Naomi hear and act upon? (See Ruth 1:6 – 7.)

    b. When Naomi set her feet toward Judah, what did she encourage her daughters-in-law to do, and why? (See Ruth 1:8 – 15.)

    c. What indication is there, based on Ruth's response, that even in Moab Naomi's family had carried out the mission God had given his people — to live in such a way as to display him to a broken world so that people outside his family would desire to know (*yadah*), or experience, God? (See Ruth 1:16 – 18.)

DID YOU KNOW?

Choices in the Face of Tragedy

In the beginning of the book of Ruth, we are introduced to the family of Elimelek from Bethlehem Ephrata of Judah. Bethlehem means "house of bread," and Ephrata (a region) means "fruitfulness." The name of Elimelek's wife, Naomi, means "pleasant" or "satisfied." These names reflect the plenty God was known to provide for his people in the land he gave to them.

Against that background, a famine raged in the land. The names of Elimelek and Naomi's sons may describe the hardships of the time: Mahlon comes from a root that means "to be sick," and Kilion from a root that means "weak." The family's response to the famine is interesting. They moved to the land of Moab across the Dead Sea, less than thirty miles away.

This decision raises the question, why? Famine prompted Abraham and Jacob to flee to Egypt where annual flooding of the Nile provided a more reliable source of water for farming than local rain. But during the exodus, God commanded his people not to return to Egypt (Deuteronomy 28:68). If Naomi and Elimelek had chosen Moab as their refuge in obedience to this command, that may explain the depth of bitterness Naomi expresses in response to the tragic losses she suffered there. Losses often can be difficult to bear when they seem to come as a result of our efforts to be faithful to God.

2. Naomi's losses must have seemed insurmountable. Nevertheless, accompanied by Ruth, she returned to the land God had given to his people. The two widows arrived in Bethlehem during the spring barley harvest, but Naomi was not the same person she was when she left Bethlehem. (See Ruth 1:19 – 22.)

   a. What had Naomi renamed herself, and why?

b. What insight into her spirit do we gain from this name change and her explanation for it?

FOR GREATER UNDERSTANDING

Naomi Becomes Marah

She started life as Naomi, meaning "satisfied" and "pleasant." But famine, death, and desperation made her life bitter, so she chose the name Marah. When applied to a person, Marah means "complete opposition, deliberately obstinate, defiant disobedience." When the women of Bethlehem began to recognize her as Naomi, the attitude of her heart poured out. "Why call me Naomi?" she challenged. "The LORD has afflicted me; the Almighty has brought misfortune upon me" (Ruth 1:21).

3. Having an attitude described as *marah* is not to be taken lightly. In the following passages of Scripture, certain phrases are derived from the root word *marah*. What insights do you gain as you consider the meaning, implications, and consequences of *marah* as used in each of the following contexts?

The Text	Translated Phrase	Meaning, Implications, Consequences
Gen. 26:34–35	source of grief	
Num. 20:24–26	rebelled	
Deut. 9:7–12	rebellious	
Deut. 21:18–21	rebellious	

4. Perhaps the best-known illustration of *marah* occurred during the exodus at a place named Marah (Exodus 15:22 – 24). The Hebrews, led by Moses (and God), had traveled for three days in the desert without finding water. They were in great distress, but the water they found at Marah was too bitter to drink. It is interesting to note that the Jewish understanding of this situation views Marah as descriptive not only of the water but of the Hebrews' hearts toward Moses and God at the time.

    a. What did God do for the Hebrews when they discovered the bitterness of the water at Marah? What did he promise them? Where did he lead them next? (See Exodus 15:25 – 27.)

    b. When they were hot, thirsty, and frightened, do you think the Hebrews had any inkling of the gracious blessings God had in store for them? Why or why not?

    c. What do you think God's intent was in leading them through that difficult and "bitter" experience?

    d. What impact do you think the experiences of Exodus 15:22 – 27 had on the attitudes of the Hebrews' hearts?

Reflection

Imagine being in Naomi and Ruth's situation, returning to Israel after God again provided food for his people there. Naomi was a survivor, but she was returning with nothing. For Ruth there was no turning back. She had left the gods of Moab behind and chosen to put her fate in the hands of Naomi's God and his people without any idea of how things would work out. What reason for hope did these destitute widows really have?

No wonder Naomi was deeply discouraged. She was certain that "the Lord's hand" had turned against her. She believed that God himself had made her life bitter. How could they have known that just the opposite was actually true? In the midst of their loss, God was orchestrating an amazing plan that generations later would affect all of humanity through the coming of God's chosen Redeemer, Jesus Christ.

> When have you, or someone you know well, experienced the feeling of being outside of God's grace — abandoned beyond the protection and provision of the *beth ab*?

> How well did you thrive on your own?

> To what extent did you struggle with attitudes of anger and bitterness against God for allowing seemingly insurmountable circumstances to surround you?

Why do you think it is so easy to become angry and embittered against God when painful circumstances arise in our lives, and why does it seem so difficult to remember and trust in his faithful love?

We know that God used the bitter water at Marah, and other circumstances of the Exodus wilderness experience, as training tools to move the Hebrews from attitudes of *marah* to obedient trust in him. In what ways has he put you through similar training in order to change your *marah* to trust in him?

Day Three | God's Provision for the Marginalized

The Very Words of God

For the LORD your God is God of gods and Lord of lords, the great God, mighty and awesome, who shows no partiality and accepts no bribes. He defends the cause of the fatherless and the widow, and loves the foreigner residing among you, giving them food and clothing. And you are to love those who are foreigners, for you yourselves were foreigners in Egypt.

Deuteronomy 10:17 – 19

Bible Discovery

A True Love Story

People often describe the book of Ruth as a love story, and certainly it contains elements of two people growing in love in the unique way of their ancient Near Eastern culture. But as this love story unfolds, we realize that it is about more than the love shared between two people. Ultimately it is about God's amazing love for all humankind, specifically his desire for his people to not only experience his love for themselves, but to reach out and display it in such a way that God is made known to his lost, hungry, and hurting children.

This story portrays the love and faithfulness Boaz demonstrated for God who, out of his love for all humankind, commands his people to care for the poor and thereby make his name known. We also see Boaz display what is in Hebrew called *hesed*, a merciful, compassionate, grace-filled loving kindness toward a foreign Moabite widow. We see Ruth's growing love and commitment to Naomi and to the God of Israel, whose amazing love was drawing Ruth into his *beth ab*.

DID YOU KNOW?
God Gave Israel a Mission

At Sinai, Israel received her mission to be a kingdom of priests and to display the nature of the Lord to the entire earth so that all people would come to know him and experience a relationship with him in the community of his people. Among those who heard God's words were Gentiles from other nations who had joined Israel and her mission. Boaz recognized that mission. It seems that he viewed Ruth — a Moabite — as an example of how God's mission was to be accomplished.

1. What do you learn from the following commands to the Hebrews about God's boundless love and passionate concern for marginalized people? Why did God especially want the Hebrews to provide for them?

   Deuteronomy 10:17 – 19

Exodus 22:22 – 27

Deuteronomy 24:14 – 15; 17 – 22

DATA FILE

Harvest Laws

God entrusted specific laws to Israel to ensure food for poor people and foreigners who lived among them. One is called *peah* ("corners") and the other is *leket* ("gleanings" or technically "waste"). As God's "partners," the Israelites were not to cut the corners of their fields or pick up what was dropped as they harvested. God's instructions did not indicate how large the uncut corners

HARVESTING GRAIN IN ANCIENT ISRAEL WAS NOT EASY. THE GRAIN HAD TO BE CUT, PILED TO DRY, AND TAKEN TO THE THRESHING FLOOR. ONLY AFTER THRESHING WAS IT READY FOR USE.

of the fields were to be or how much grain might be dropped. His people were to decide those matters according to their own hearts.

In ancient Israel, the land, its produce, and the means of production belonged to the Lord; thus it was to be used to honor him in the way he desired. It was each owner's family responsibility to recognize it had more than it needed and to be generous. If the family obeyed, God promised to continually provide more than was needed so that marginalized people would be cared for within the community. If the community falsely believed its wealth to be its own rather than God's and began withholding the "corners" and the "gleanings," then the marginalized would suffer.

Although there was no dishonor in being poor, marginalized people also had to do back-breaking work to receive their provisions. They gathered, threshed, winnowed, sifted, ground, and baked — just as those who had plenty. This partnership that God established with his people before they ever set foot in the Promised Land is what saved Naomi and Ruth from starvation.

2. When Ruth and Naomi returned to Bethlehem, they had no means of support. But God had already put in place provision for them — the opportunity to glean in the fields during harvest. In fact, Boaz and Ruth first met when Ruth was gleaning in a field that belonged to Boaz. Read Ruth 2:4 – 16.

    a. What do you notice about the way Boaz carried out his God-given responsibility to care for those in need who were outside the "father's house"?

    b. How aware do you think Boaz was of his responsibility to be God's provision — and ultimately God's "partner" in providing protection, provision, and shelter for Ruth as a foreign widow? Why?

   c. How did Ruth respond to the blessings she was receiving in the community of the Lord, and how do you think it influenced her desire to fully embrace the God of Naomi and his people?

3. Although the standards of measure differ, scholars have noted that the generous amount of grain Ruth gleaned (Ruth 2:17) approximates the amount Abraham and Sarah offered the three strangers (Genesis 18:6). What might this detail suggest about what may have guided Boaz in obediently showing his faithfulness to God?

DID YOU REALIZE?

When Ruth appeared to glean in the fields of Boaz, he greeted her—a pagan foreigner and outsider—warmly as "daughter" and took immediate action to go beyond what the Torah commanded. Not only did he provide water and shelter, he invited her to eat with the harvesters (probably members of his extended family) and told them to increase the size of the *leket* (dropped portion). He also invited her to return to his family plot all through the harvest, apparently intending to extend his generosity even further. These generous offers displayed his faithfulness in obeying not only the letter but the intent of God's instructions to protect and provide for the disenfranchised.

Reflection

Remember!

More than two hundred times in Scripture, God calls his people to "remember." In English usage, *remember* means "to mentally recall" or "to cognitively bring to mind." The Hebrew word *zakar* means more than recollection. It refers to mental activity that leads to a response; it is to recall *and* to act. The Bible uses *zakar* to refer to God's "remembering." When God remembers, he does more than recall; he acts accordingly. So to ask God to remember is to ask God to act in a certain way.

In Deuteronomy 15:15, God commanded his people to "remember" that they had been redeemed. This was not simply a request to think about their past. It was a call to act in response to the price God had paid to deliver them from trouble so that they could be fully restored to his community. They were to remember their redemption and respond by living faithfully as God was teaching them.

It is no different for God's redeemed people today. God expects us to be agents of redemption in the lives of others. We are to remember what God has done — not just for us but throughout redemptive history. Then we are to act and reach out to those who are marginalized because we are God's provision for them. We are God's partners who make known his character and love so those who are lost may be restored fully — spiritually, socially, economically — to the community of God's people.

> Boaz apparently remembered two things that led him to respond as he did to Ruth's desperate need: he remembered God's commands for providing for those in need, and he remembered how generously Abraham and Sarah provided for the strangers at their tent. As you remember these things, how do they instruct you in responding faithfully to the needs of people around you in ways that put God's love for them on display?

What other commands, stories, or people in the Bible are important for you to remember and act upon so that you can love those who are alienated from God in ways that welcome them into the Father's house? Write them down, and *remember*!

What difference does it make in terms of your love, concern, generosity, and compassion for those who do not know God when you remember yourself as a child who also was lost in sin and in need of redemption?

What did God provide in your life experience when you were still alienated from him that led you to recognize his love for you and to desire to know him and his redemption? How does remembering (and acting according to) those experiences help you to engage as an agent of redemption with those who are outside the community of God?

Day Four | God Raises up a Kinsman Redeemer

The Very Words of God

> *Boaz replied, "I've been told all about what you have done for your mother-in-law since the death of your husband — how you left your father and mother and your homeland and came to live with a people*

*you did not know before. May the L*ORD *repay you for what you have done. May you be richly rewarded by the L*ORD*, the God of Israel, under whose wings you have come to take refuge."*

Ruth 2:11 – 12

Bible Discovery

Boaz: Devoted to Fulfilling His Responsibilities

In the patriarchal culture of ancient Israel, the Torah required the "kinsman redeemer" (sometimes translated "guardian redeemer") to bear the responsibility for the well-being of his extended family. He was legally obligated to redeem relatives in serious difficulty, to ensure that needy members of the kin group were cared for, to redeem (restore) any lost property from those who owned or leased it to the family that had lost it, and even was expected to provide an heir for a man who had died childless.

1. Naomi knew God's commands regarding redemption or restoration of a destitute widow (Leviticus 25:25 – 28, 35 – 38;
   Deuteronomy 25:5 – 10). She knew that a member of the family of her deceased husband was obligated to provide for her
   and for Ruth as her daughter-in-law, and she recognized Boaz
   as a kinsman.

   a. What plan to claim her redemption did Naomi put into
      motion for Ruth, a childless widow, in order to continue
      Elimelek's family line in Israel? (See Ruth 3:1 – 4.)

   b. How did Ruth respond to Naomi's instructions? (See
      Ruth 3:5 – 9.)

DATA FILE
Threshing Grain

In ancient Israel, harvesters cut barley by hand, tied it into small bundles, and piled it near a threshing floor to dry. A typical threshing floor was a flat rock surface, usually surrounded by a low wall, on a high place exposed to the wind. Since a threshing floor was not necessarily close to the homes where people lived, some family members might sleep at the threshing floor in order to protect their food supply until the harvest was complete.

Dry grain was spread on the floor where a threshing sled, which looked a bit like a toboggan with stones embedded in the bottom, was used to separate the kernels from the husks. Typically family members (often children) rode the sled as a donkey pulled it over the grain. This caused the kernels to separate but remain mixed with stalks and husks. On a windy day, family members used small pitchforks to throw the mixture into the air. Wind blew the lighter chaff (husks and stalks) off to the side to be gathered for use in the family oven. The heavier kernels of grain fell to the threshing floor where they were gathered up, sifted with a screen to remove additional impurities, and stored in jars.

AN ANCIENT STONE THRESHING FLOOR AND A TYPICAL THRESHING SLED. WINNOWING ALLOWS GRAIN TO BE GATHERED APART FROM THE STALKS AND CHAFF.

AFTER THRESHING AND WINNOWING, THE GRAIN WAS STONE-GROUND.

2. Boaz was certainly surprised by Ruth's nighttime presence at the threshing floor. Yet her actions and her request, although they may seem odd to us, made perfect sense to him. As her kinsman redeemer, he responded graciously and appropriately in every way. Read Ruth 3:8 – 4:12 as well as "Did You Know?"

DID YOU KNOW?

"Uncover His Feet"

Much has been written about what Ruth actually did when she uncovered the feet of Boaz and lay down at the threshing floor (Ruth 3:7). The phrase is a euphemism that had sexual overtones in the culture and in the Bible (Exodus 4:25). Boaz and Ruth are presented as righteous people, and there is no suggestion of any sexual impropriety in this story. Yet the act of "uncovering his *feet*" and lying "at his *feet*" communicated to Boaz his responsibility within his covenant with the Lord, as symbolized by his circumcision, to become her redeemer.

Ruth's request to "spread the corner of your garment over me" had several meanings, each of which highlighted her desire to be a faithful part of the community of God's people. God had commanded his people to sew tassels on the corners of their garments as a constant reminder of their covenant to obey God's commands. The word for "corner" in Hebrew also means "wings," so Ruth was asking Boaz: "Protect me like a bird protects her young; be my redeemer as God commanded in the Torah so that in your actions, your provision, and your family I will find God's protection; and take me as your wife for in your protection I will find God's provision and protection."

a. How did Boaz respond to Ruth's request, and how did he honor her in his response? (See Ruth 3:10 – 13.)

    b. By agreeing to spread his garment over her, Boaz was saying to Ruth, "As I faithfully before God seek to provide for you and care for you, may you find the protection of God's wings." What did his gift of six measures of barley — more than a person could normally carry — say about his desire to obey God and his commitment to Ruth? (See Genesis 18:2 – 8; Ruth 3:15 – 18.)

DATA FILE

The Town or City Gate

In the ancient world, the town or city gate was the commercial, judicial, religious, and social center of the city. It was where pagan kings demonstrated how well their gods could defeat the forces of chaos, including poverty and hunger. A community that could provide for needy people was considered to have powerful gods.

In the Torah, God provided instructions about caring for the poor who were "in the gate": "Rob not the poor, because he is poor: neither oppress the afflicted in the gate" (Proverbs 22:22, KJV). Whether Israel followed the cultural pattern literally and cared for people by the gate or God was using the idea as a metaphor, the gate represented the Lord's justice and compassion for those in need. Thus Boaz went to the gate for legal reasons and to ensure that Ruth and Naomi would be cared for properly.

    3. Taking the role of kinsman redeemer in Ruth and Naomi's situation was not a simple matter for Boaz because another man was actually more closely related to the family than he. So he went to the city gate, where the elders gathered and legal matters of the community were settled, and approached the unnamed redeemer.

a. What was the anonymous redeemer willing to do? What did he refuse to do, and why? (See Ruth 4:2 – 6.)

b. How did the audience in the gate respond to Boaz's declaration of redemption, and how aware were they of God's providence through Boaz? (See Ruth 4:7 – 12.)

FOR GREATER UNDERSTANDING
Finding a Faithful Redeemer

By law Naomi still held the right of redemption to get back her land — the "inheritance," *nahala*, that God had given the family when they entered the Promised Land — from whoever now owned or leased it.

It's unclear why the unnamed redeemer believed that redeeming Naomi's property *and* marrying Ruth would endanger his *nahala*. Perhaps if he had a son by Ruth and that son was his only heir, his own inheritance would go to Elimelek and Naomi's family. Or, perhaps a son by Ruth would receive the land he bought back in the name of Ruth's deceased husband, Mahlon. In any case, he refused to fulfill his obligations as a redeemer.

Although we might assume that Boaz was wealthy because he hired harvesters and is described as a "man of standing" (Ruth 2:1), Jewish thought prefers to understand that Boaz was a man of moral character — a man of valor. Hence his legal responsibility to redeem Naomi's land likely required significant sacrifice.

4. How did God restore Naomi and Ruth to the community of his people, and how did God use Ruth — a former Moabite outcast (see Deuteronomy 23:3) and one of the first Gentiles to join God's people[2] in his ongoing plan of redemption? (See Ruth 4:13 – 17; Matthew 1:1 – 16.)

Reflection

Boaz and Ruth are a beautiful example of the way that redemption worked in a patriarchal culture. God included the practice of redemption, common in ancient Near Eastern culture, in his instructions to the Israelites. In so doing, he explained his role as "Father" (or patriarch) of all and his desire to redeem family members and the entire creation, restoring them fully in relationship to him and to each other. Thus the righteous and faithful character of Boaz is a picture of God himself in his work of redemption.

After God used Israel to bring Ruth fully into his community, she joined in the mission to redeem others. She became the great-grandmother of Israel's heroic king, David, demonstrating that a foreigner could be completely assimilated into God's people and become his instrument for redemptive purpose. Jesus' descent from David's family in both blood through his mother, Mary, and legal kinship through his father, Joseph, gave him legitimacy as Messiah to Israel among his first Jewish followers. Jesus' descent from Ruth made it clear that the Messiah would redeem all humanity, not only the Jews.

For Christians, the book of Ruth represents an early sign that the Messiah would liberate all of humankind, not solely Jews, and that Gentiles would join God's community of redeemed people in the mission of restoring God's lost children back into full relationship with him. Think of the honor given to God and the blessings we'd receive if we took seriously his desire to redeem those outside his *beth ab.*

Restoring lost people to his community is so important that God sent his Son to die to pay the debt for their redemption.

> In grateful response to the gift God has given you, take time out to identify, pray about, and act upon the ways God may want you to "spend yourself" to further his mission of redemption and restoration.

Memorize

> *If you spend yourselves in behalf of the hungry and satisfy the needs of
> the oppressed, then your light will rise in the darkness, and your night
> will become like the noonday.*
> *The Lord will guide you always; he will satisfy your needs in a sun-
> scorched land and will strengthen your frame. You will be like a well-
> watered garden, like a spring whose waters never fail.*

Isaiah 58:10 – 11

Day Five | Hosea and Gomer: Seeking the Lost

The Very Words of God

> *The Lord said to me, "Go, show your love to your wife again, though she
> is loved by another man and is an adulteress. Love her as the Lord loves
> the Israelites, though they turn to other gods and love the sacred raisin
> cakes." So I bought her for fifteen shekels of silver and about a homer
> and a lethek of barley.*

Hosea 3:1 – 2

Bible Discovery

A Tireless Redeemer

The book of Hosea tells the story of the holy Hebrew prophet Hosea
and his adulterous wife, Gomer. Prominent in the story are Hosea's
faithful, tireless efforts to restore his marginalized wife to the protection and care of his *beth ab* — the "father's house." The story provides another significant biblical example of a redeemer (*go'el*) and
expands our picture of what redemption (*ga'al*) entails. Not only
does the story challenge us to greater faithfulness, it illustrates God's
desire to redeem his lost children and for them, in turn, to become
agents of his redemption in the world.

1. During the final days of Israel's northern kingdom, in the
   eighth century BC, God commissioned Hosea to live as a picture of what was happening in God's relationship with his
   chosen bride, Israel. Read Hosea 1 – 3.

    a. What did God command Hosea to do, and what impact do you imagine his actions had on his reputation among his neighbors as a prophet of God? (See Hosea 1:2 – 9.)

    b. What point was God making concerning his desire to seek out and restore his people, Israel, through the example of Gomer and her sexually immoral lifestyle? (See Ezekiel 20:6 – 12.)

2. Hosea redeemed Gomer and provided for her in his safe, loving *beth ab*. She went from being a despised, abused outcast to being the beloved wife of a respected prophet and the mother of three children. But the pull of her past was strong. What did Gomer do that took her back outside of the *beth ab* — and no doubt deeply hurt and shamed her godly husband? (See Hosea 3:1.)

    a. Eventually Gomer hit the bottom of life outside God's house; she was put up for sale as a sex slave. What did God command Hosea to do, despite his wife's sinfulness, in order to restore her through grace to his loving community and to wholeness? (See Hosea 3:1 – 2.)

    b. What does the example of Hosea's faithful pursuit of his wayward wife reveal to you about God's heart for his lost children and the price God is willing to pay to bring us back into his loving family — even when we stray in pursuit of the "pleasures" of our sinful world? (See Romans 5:8; 1 John 1:9.)

c. What does this story indicate about the cost in terms of resources or reputation that may be required of those who commit to being instruments of God's redemption for those who are outside the protection and provision of God's house?

3. To whom has God the Father entrusted the responsibility of seeking the lost and restoring them to the Father's house, and who are the family members in his *beth ab*? (See John 14:1 – 3; Colossians 1:13 – 15, 18 – 20; Ephesians 2:13, 19 – 22.)

THINK ABOUT IT

To Be a Hosea

It would have been scandalous for a man of God like Hosea to even consider redeeming a woman like Gomer. She was an outcast, a woman with no future. She probably would never have had a husband, and the community would have spurned her and any children she bore.

Then God intervened in the person of Hosea, who redeemed her, made her his wife, and loved her! No longer a despised outcast, unworthy of being a wife, she found her life filled with God's blessings. Her place in the *beth ab* was a miracle of grace she experienced every day!

When she again chose an immoral lifestyle, she was even lower than before. Eventually she was auctioned as a sex slave, and brought only half the normal price of a slave (see Exodus 21:32; Hosea 3:2). Imagine Hosea's grief and shame when he stood before his community and bought her back. Imagine the gossip, the shaking heads, the questions. What an expression of God's love! What a personal price he paid!

Like Gomer, each of us is an unworthy sinner whom God has sought to bring out of darkness and into the light and love of his *beth ab*. Jesus paid the full debt of our unfaithfulness to redeem us. Although our tendency is to seek out other lovers, God is amazing. He is faithful to seek us out and restore us to his house as Hosea did for Gomer and the Lord did for Israel.

Like Hosea, God intends for each of us to be nurtured and blessed within the context of his family and to become instruments of his redemption in our world. Regardless of the cost in resources or reputation, God calls us to seek those who are outside the protection and provision of the Father's house. Like Hosea, we are to seek out the Gomers of our world.

Reflection

The immediate intent of the story of Hosea and Gomer was to address the condition of the relationship between God and his "bride," Israel. But its message is not limited to that situation. It also describes the great personal sacrifice and effort Hosea put forth to restore his marginalized wife to the *beth ab,* the "father's house." And it reminds us that all of us have been unworthy sinners outside God's family. Yet God spared no effort to seek us out and no expense to redeem us. By his grace and loving kindness, he brought us out of our spiritual darkness and restored us into his family — the household of faith.

God desires for us to be nurtured and blessed within the context of his family. But his desire for the lost doesn't end with us. We are surrounded by a world of spiritually lost people; God wants us to be faithful instruments of his blessing and redemption wherever we are and whatever our situation may be. Our willingness to partner with God in seeking spiritually lost people is in part motivated by our awareness of God's merciful compassion and the grace he extended to us.

How much have you thought about the price God paid to restore you to his family?

How deeply must God love you to have paid that price?

How are you showing your appreciation to God for what he has done to bring you into the protection and provision of his *beth ab*?

God's very nature is to be deeply concerned for those who are outside the protection of his *beth ab*. This underlies the seriousness of the mission that he entrusts to his people — to seek out the marginalized, the broken, the oppressed, and those in bondage and to be agents of God's redemption so they can be fully restored to the family of God.

How willing are you to expend your resources and time to seek out God's lost children and help to restore them to God's community?

It could not have been easy for Hosea to seek out Gomer the first time, and certainly not the second time. How willing are you to seek out God's lost children, even if others misunderstand or look down on you for doing so?

Think of people you encounter through your daily life who are outside the family of God. Make a list of them and the ways in which they are marginalized, suffering, or in bondage to sin.

Begin identifying specific actions you might take in order to be an instrument of God's redemption in their lives. Think of ways you can put God on display so that they will desire to be restored to the Father's house.

Consider how you and others in your faith community can join together in seeking out God's lost children and displaying for them the love, protection, and provision available to everyone who is redeemed and brought into his household.

Memorize

Then Jesus told them this parable: "Suppose one of you has a hundred sheep and loses one of them. Doesn't he leave the ninety-nine in the open country and go after the lost sheep until he finds it? And when he finds it, he joyfully puts it on his shoulders and goes home. Then he calls his friends and neighbors together and says, 'Rejoice with me; I have found my lost sheep.'"

Luke 15:3 – 6

ISRAEL AT SINAI: THE FIRST GREAT COMMISSION

Israel's encounter with God at the foot of Mount Sinai — the mountain of God — is the formative moment in her relationship with him. It is the foundation that resonates throughout the course of the Bible story — from its rumblings before the days of the exodus through the apostle John's vision of a future new creation. At Mount Sinai the Lord established a partnership with his people through which he would restore *shalom* to a creation reeling in chaos because of humanity's rebellion against God the Creator. That partnership between God and his people, who were called to live in faithful covenant with him, would pave the way for the redemption of all humanity!

The year the Hebrews spent at the foot of Mount Sinai was as significant to their identity as any event in their history. If we are to understand God's plan for his creation and the role he desires his people to play in it, we must spend time with his ancient people at Sinai:

- Where God gave meaning and purpose to their bitter years of slavery and their dramatic deliverance from oppression.
- Where God began to refine and shape their identity as a holy nation, a kingdom of priests, partners in covenant with him.
- Where God called them to a mission of eternal consequence.

That mission is the focus of this study.[1] God put his people on the crossroads of the ancient world where all nations could see them. He then commissioned them to be his witnesses to the world, mak-

ing his name — his reputation, his identity, his character — known
to all nations. God intended that they accomplish this mission not
so much by telling others about him but by living in such a way that
the eyes and ears of all people would be opened to know and worship him. They were not just to *bring* the message, they were to *be*
the message.

We must realize that the Israelites were not called to a life of service
to God in order to obtain redemption. That came by God's grace
alone. God desired for his people, as a kingdom of priests, to live
such righteous lives that other people would come to know him as
their Redeemer and Lord. The Bible records many examples of Israel's devotion to the Lord through which others came to know him.
Yet Israel often was unfaithful — either by being so much like their
pagan neighbors that they had no distinct witness of their God or
by being so set apart that they had little or no contact with those to
whom they were sent to be witnesses.

So God sent his Son, Jesus the Messiah, to be that witness to Israel
and to the rest of the world. Yes, Jesus is the Lamb of God our
Redeemer; he also came to call Israel back to her mission of being
a kingdom of priests to the nations. His repeated debates with religious Jews of his day concerning his contact with "sinners" are
examples of this message (Matthew 9:10 – 13; Mark 2:15 – 17; Luke
15:1 – 7).

Jesus also chose twelve disciples (an allusion to the twelve tribes
of Israel that first received God's commission to be his kingdom of
priests) whom he commissioned to be his witnesses to Israel and
to be like Israel to all nations (see Acts 1:8). Today that royal priesthood comprises all people who follow Jesus. We are commissioned,
as Israel was at Mount Sinai, to stand between God and a world in
chaos and proclaim the knowledge of God through our words and
by how we live so that others will experience his redemption and
restoration. By considering the mission God gave to ancient Israel,
we gain a better understanding of the responsibilities of the royal
priesthood that is the community of Jesus.

Opening Thoughts (3 minutes)

The Very Words of God

> *Then Moses went up to God, and the LORD called to him from the mountain and said, "This is what you are to say to the descendants of Jacob and what you are to tell the people of Israel: 'You yourselves have seen what I did to Egypt, and how I carried you on eagles' wings and brought you to myself. Now if you obey me fully and keep my covenant, then out of all nations you will be my treasured possession. Although the whole earth is mine, you will be for me a kingdom of priests and a holy nation.'"*

Exodus 19:3 – 6

Think About It

Every human relationship has defining moments — shared experiences or meaningful interaction — that clarify and shape the future of that relationship. Often the response to these moments moves the participants toward a more intimate relationship. Sometimes these moments create distance in the relationship that can lead to its demise.

God created people for relationship with him, so there are defining moments in our relationship with God as well. What have been some of the pivotal, defining moments in your relationship with God? What lasting impact have they had on your relationship with him?

DVD Notes (32 minutes)

God gives his people a mission

Why the desert and Mount Sinai?

The kingdom where God reigns
    Where God is obeyed

    Where God's will is done

Good news! The God of Israel reigns

Set apart as priests to show what God is like

DVD Discussion (7 minutes)

1. Before reaching Mount Sinai, the Hebrews had been released from generations of slavery in Egypt and for forty days had endured the hardships of desert travel.

   a.   What do you think it was like for them to be removed from the only life they had known in the lush Nile Valley, led far away into a vast, barren desert, and then to experience God's awesome power and majesty at the mountain?

   b.   What might they have thought when they learned that God had chosen *them* — of all people — to be in an intimate relationship with him and to be his partners in the mission of redeeming all of humanity?

THIS ARTIST'S RENDERING OF GOD'S "KINGDOM OF PRIESTS" AT MOUNT SINAI CAPTURES THE POWERFUL IMAGE OF A MOUNTAIN IN THE SINAI DESERT AND HELPS US TO PICTURE THE STUNNING EVENTS OF GOD'S COMMISSION OF ISRAEL.

2. We tend to think of kingdoms in terms of geographical space, but God defines his kingdom — the territory where he reigns — in terms of what happens when his will is done. In what ways does this change in perception alter your understanding of what is required to be his partner in restoring *shalom* to a world in chaos?

3. How do you think people around you would describe what God's reign looks like? Do they see it as peace, good tidings, salvation — or something else?

    What changes in the way you live could better demonstrate God's mercy, love, and kindness?

FOR GREATER UNDERSTANDING
The Geography of the Exodus
The location of Mount Sinai (Horeb, mountain of God) and the route the Hebrews took to get there is one of the most debated geographical issues of the Bible. Although the Torah precisely and clearly describes the exodus from Egypt and names specific locations during the journey to and after leaving Mount Sinai, archaeological information on these sites is insufficient to resolve the debate.

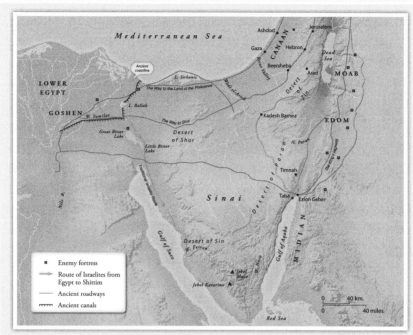

THE EXODUS AND THE SINAI PENINSULA

Nearly all scholars agree on the route the Hebrews did not take: "the road through the Philistine country." That route, along the Mediterranean coast on the northwestern edge of the Sinai Peninsula, was part of the ancient trade route and military road between Egypt and Canaan that eventually went all the way to the Tigris and Euphrates Rivers and the land of Babylon. The Text itself says, "When Pharaoh let the people go, God did not lead them on the road through the Philistine country, though that was shorter. For God said, 'If they face war, they might change their minds and return to Egypt'" (Exodus 13:17).

Significant Jewish and Christian scholars have presented evidence for at least twenty locations of Mount Sinai and argued three major theories regarding the route the Israelites took after leaving Egypt: southern Jordan or northwest Saudi Arabia; northern Sinai Peninsula; and the traditional location in the mountains of southern Sinai.

The goal of our study is to explore biblical events within their historical-cultural context so that we can better understand God's revelation through them, not to make a case for a particular geographical theory. We choose locations because of their typical desert features—wells, mountains, vegetation, topography, roads—that portray the locations mentioned in the Text. Those who are interested in understanding evidence for particular locations or routes would be well served to seek sources that have this as their intent.[2]

For filming this study, we chose Mount Timnah in the Desert of Paran to gain a sense of the setting for the momentous events when God commissioned his "kingdom of priests" at Mount Sinai. Mount Timnah is located in southern Israel, at the northern end of the Sinai Desert along the route the Israelites took when they first approached the Promised Land. It is not where the events of God giving the Torah occurred. However, those events happened in the same desert region and Mount Timnah is similar in appearance to the traditional Mount Sinai site.

Small Group Bible Discovery and Discussion (13 minutes)

God Takes a Suitable Helper for Himself

Many people recognize Mount Sinai as the location where God gave the Ten Commandments to Moses, but most, even among those who call themselves Christians, fail to recognize the significance of what took place between God and his people there. To some, the Ten Commandments are merely a list of God's dos and don'ts. Few realize that the Ten Commandments are a brief summary of the formative, life-changing covenant God established with his people at Mount Sinai.

That covenant defined and affirmed God's relationship with Israel. Similar to the way God gave Eve to be Adam's suitable helper in caring for his creation, God claimed Israel to be his suitable helper in the mission of redemption. Although the Text does not specifically label God's revelation of the covenant on Mount Sinai as a wedding, the language and customs of marriage in ancient times appear throughout the story. The marriage language used highlights the love and intimacy God desired in his relationship with Israel. The image conveyed is that at Mount Sinai the Lord took Israel to be his bride!

1. In Exodus 6:7, God says to Moses and the Israelites, "I will
    take you as my own." The Hebrew word used in this phrase,
    laqakh, describes taking a wife for oneself or for another
    person. So according to Jewish thought, God viewed his
    relationship with Israel as a covenant of marriage and the
    experiences at Mount Sinai as a wedding. What insights do
    the following verses contribute to your understanding of this
    "marriage" relationship?

    Exodus 19:3 – 6

    Deuteronomy 7:6 – 9

    Isaiah 54:5

    Jeremiah 2:1 – 2

    Jeremiah 31:32

DID YOU KNOW?

A "covenant" is an agreement between two parties in which both promise under oath to perform or refrain from certain actions described in advance. More than just a legal agreement, a covenant signifies a permanent bond between people. Covenants were common in the culture of the Bible, and the covenants in the Text are remarkably similar to cultural agreements. These were of varying types, including those between equal and unequal parties.

Covenant is a major metaphor for the relations between God and his people. God made a covenant with Abraham to make him the father of a great nation that would bring God's blessing to others and to give his descendants a land in which to live and make God known. This covenant was confirmed by blood sacrifice. God's agreement with Israel at Mount Sinai was also a covenant that sealed the relationship between God and his chosen people. This covenant was summarized in the Ten Commandments written on stone tablets.[3]

2. At times God's marriage relationship with Israel blossomed. Many biblical characters were passionately faithful in their love for God (Joshua, Rahab, Ruth, David, Hezekiah, Samuel, Elijah, Esther). Others (Saul, Ahab, Jezebel, Jeroboam) were unfaithful to the Lord — their husband — and pursued other gods. Read 1 Chronicles 5:24 – 25; Jeremiah 3:6 – 10; and Ezekiel 16:8 – 22.

    a. Which powerful words and images did the prophets use to describe the idolatry of God's people?

    b. How does the prophets' portrayal of idolatry in terms of marital unfaithfulness reinforce the idea that the events of Mount Sinai were a wedding?

3. It is important to realize that God did not simply give Israel a mission at Mount Sinai. He established an intimate relationship with his people by which they would share in the mission of blessing and redeeming all nations. He chose them to be his kingdom of priests, a community that experienced him intimately and out of love for their "husband" would live according to his righteousness. That kingdom of priests was, and is, God's suitable helper — his bride!

    a. What mission did God give to Adam and Eve (the "suitable helper" God provided for him), and why do you think it was important for Adam to have someone with whom to share that mission? (See Genesis 1:27 - 28; 2:15 - 20.)

    b. Read Exodus 19:5 - 6 and Deuteronomy 26:16 - 19 and talk about the impact the partnership God envisioned with his "suitable helper" would have on restoring *shalom* to a world that did not know him.

4. How would Israel maintain an intimate relationship with God so that she would continue to be a suitable helper in the mission of restoring *shalom* to his lost creation? (See Deuteronomy 10:12 - 21; 11:13 - 21.)

DID YOU KNOW?
The Most Valued of All Possessions
Ancient texts, including the Bible, use the term "treasured possession" (Hebrew: *segulah*[4]) to describe a king's personal treasures — the select objects that were most precious to him. Although a king valued all his possessions, his *segulah* was more carefully protected than all the others and often was displayed for everyone to see. So imagine what it meant when God chose Israel to be his "treasured possession" (Deuteronomy 14:2; 26:18).

The use of *segulah* to describe God's special covenant relationship with Israel indicates the depth of his love for his people. God chose Israel not because of any qualities that had made the Hebrews so "loveable" or because of anything they had done. He chose them as a loving act of his heart and will. By claiming Israel as his *segulah,* he was in a sense saying, "You will always be my beloved. I will always love you with my whole heart. To experience that love, you must stay in faithful relationship with me, maintaining the relationship I have established with you." Israel's love and faithfulness was the expected response to God's act of naming them as his *segulah*.

Faith Lesson (4 minutes)

At Mount Sinai, God gave meaning and purpose to his people's bitter slavery in Egypt and their dramatic deliverance. The exodus experience emphasizes Israel's status as God's chosen people. They would be his bride with whom he would live and share in the mission of restoring *shalom* to his world. But their story began long before they left Egypt, long before their ancestors even went to Egypt. Their story was a continuation of the promise God made to Abraham that his descendants would bring God's blessing to the world. Take a few minutes to review the "back story" to what happened at Sinai, and plan to study it more in depth on your own. It will help you see the big picture of God's plan of redemption.

What God Did to Bring a People to Himself	The Text
Chose Abraham to be father of a people who would be agents of God's blessing to the world.	Gen. 12:1–3
Gave Abraham the land of Canaan and promised that after a time of enslavement in Egypt his descendants would live there and carry out God's mission to the world.	Gen. 15:7–19
Established an eternal relationship with Abraham and his descendants by making a covenant with him.	Gen. 17:3–8
The sons of Jacob, Abraham's grandson, became Israel's twelve tribes. Through God's providence, one of the sons, Joseph, delivered the family from famine in Canaan by moving them to Egypt.	Gen. 27–32; 37; 39–47; 48:1–4; 50
God blessed Israel in Egypt, but his plan was for them to live in Canaan. When a new pharaoh oppressed Israel brutally, the people cried out to God (*ze'akah*).	Ex. 1:6–7; 2:23–24
God raised up Moses, having prepared him to lead his enslaved people to freedom and the Promised Land.	Ex. 2
Having heard the *ze'akah* of his people, God appeared to Moses and commissioned him to lead Israel to freedom.	Ex. 3–4
God made himself known to the Hebrews, Egyptians, and the world when, through ten powerful plagues, he demonstrated his power over each of Egypt's gods.	Ex. 5–12
When Pharaoh refused to let God's firstborn, Israel, worship him, God demanded the life of Egypt's firstborn. After God rescued his people at the Reed (Red) Sea, they put their faith in him and his servant Moses.	Ex. 4:21–23; 11–12:30; 14–15:21
Through Moses, God kept reminding Israel of his faithfulness to his promises.	Ex. 3:6, 15–16; 4:1–5; 6:2–8
For forty days God led Israel through the desert wilderness by fire and by cloud. By the power of his mighty arm he miraculously provided for them, bringing them safely to Mount Sinai.	Ex. 6:6; 13:20–22; 15:22–19:2
Israel camped at the foot of the mountain of God where, true to his word, God met with Moses.	Ex. 3:12; 19

At Mount Sinai, God gave his people the "great commission" to be his partners in extending his blessing to all nations as he had promised Abraham. That commission to Israel is the basis for the mission God gave to Jesus. It is also the basis for the mission Jesus gave to his disciples in Galilee before he returned to heaven (Matthew 28:16–20). The mission to be a "kingdom of priests" that brings God's blessing to a broken world is the mission God continues to entrust to his people today.

FOR GREATER UNDERSTANDING
God Calls a "Kingdom of Priests"

During biblical times, God's people lived among cultures that worshiped many gods, each of which had its own priesthood. The privilege of interacting with the god or its statue was open only to the priest who served as the mediator between the god and the people. The priest was a representation of the god and acted on behalf of the god, so to meet and observe the priest was in a sense to meet the god.

The Bible uses the concept of a "priesthood" to describe the mission God has given to his people. In the Hebrew Bible, Exodus 19:5–6 establishes a "kingdom of priests": " 'Now if you obey me fully and keep my covenant, then out of all nations you will be my treasured possession. Although the whole earth is mine, you will be for me a kingdom of priests and a holy nation.' These are the words you are to speak to the Israelites."

In the Christian Text, 1 Peter 2:9, 12 describes "a chosen people, a royal priesthood, a holy nation, God's special possession, that you may declare the praises of him who called you out of darkness into his wonderful light … Live such good lives among the pagans that, though they accuse you of doing wrong, they may see your good deeds and glorify God on the day he visits us."

At Sinai and through Peter's epistle God instructs his people to be his "priests" to the whole world. The nature of the mission is for God's people to serve God and humanity by demonstrating in words and actions the will and character of God. They are not only commissioned to bring the message but to be the message in everything they do. In the ancient world, a kingdom was any situation in which the king—in this case, God—was obeyed. So a kingdom of priests is a community of people who live by God's commands and thereby display him to the world around them. By interacting with God's people, his "priesthood," the people of the world come to know God.

1. What richness in our experience with God do we miss if we focus on only part of the biblical story rather than the whole?

2. In what ways has your understanding of the scope of God's mission to redeem the world — from the time of Abraham to this day — grown by what you have studied in this session? And how will you respond to that greater understanding?

3. What does it mean to you that God considers you to be his partner in accomplishing this great mission?

4. If you were to view yourself as a "suitable helper," a chosen, intimate partner with God in making him known to people outside his *beth ab,* what changes would you make in how you live out God's message to the world?

Closing (1 minute)

Read together Deuteronomy 7:6, 9: "For you are a people holy to the LORD your God. The LORD your God has chosen you out of all the peoples on the face of the earth to be his people, his treasured possession ... Know therefore that the LORD your God is God; he is the faithful God, keeping his covenant of love to a thousand generations of those who love him and keep his commandments."

Then pray, thanking God for his love for all who are lost. Praise him for his faithfulness in keeping the covenant he made at Sinai. Thank him for choosing you to be his partner in the great mission of restoring *shalom* to his creation. Express your commitment, as his beloved, to be faithful in every way and ask him to forgive you when you are not.

Memorize

> *For you are a people holy to the LORD your God. The LORD your God has chosen you out of all the peoples on the face of the earth to be his people, his treasured possession.... Know therefore that the LORD your God is God; he is the faithful God, keeping his covenant of love to a thousand generations of those who love him and keep his commandments.*
>
> *Deuteronomy 7:6, 9*

Restoring the Lost to the Father's House

In-Depth Personal Study Sessions

Day One | God Lives with His People!

The Very Words of God

> *I will dwell among the Israelites and be their God. They will know that I am the* Lord *their God, who brought them out of Egypt so that I might dwell among them. I am the* Lord *their God.*

> **Exodus 29:45 – 46**

Bible Discovery

God Comes to Live with His Kingdom of Priests

God's ardent desire has always been to be present with his people. He was physically present in the Garden of Eden with Adam and Eve, his partners in caring for his creation. The intimacy of that relationship was shattered by sin, broken by Adam and Eve's unfaithfulness in keeping God's commands. But God's desire was to again establish an intimate, covenant relationship with the people he created and to live among them as he had at the beginning. The covenant he made with Israel at Mount Sinai would provide such a place for God to live.

1. After God finished his creation, Genesis 3:8 portrays God and his beloved human partners "walking" together in the Garden of Eden. We should note that the Hebrew word translated "walk" is *halak,* which usually means "to live." So it appears that God's dwelling place was in heaven as well as on earth in intimate relationship with Adam and Eve. What created distance in the relationship between God and his human partners that prevented him from living with them? (See Genesis 3:6 – 13, 22 – 24.)

2. Although God is holy and could no longer live in community with his human partners, he never gave up on the
   relationship. From time to time, as revealed in the following accounts, God appeared to and communicated with
   his people. What was his purpose in these appearances,
   and what do they reveal about the kind of relationship he
   desired? (See Genesis 17:1 – 8; 26:2 – 5; Exodus 3:1 – 10;
   34:4 – 10.)

3. God brought his people to Mount Sinai where he claimed
   Israel as his bride, establishing a covenant that they would
   be his partners in relationship forever. But that intimate partnership was not an end in itself.

   a. What did God ask his people to build so that he would
      have a suitable place to live among them, and why was
      this important in light of their mission? (See Exodus
      25:8; 29:44 – 45.)

   b. How do we know that God's presence was restored
      to his people and, through them, to a broken world —
      through the place his people made for him to live? (See
      Leviticus 9:22 – 24.)

4. When God commissioned Israel to be his "kingdom of priests" (Exodus 19:3 – 6), his people understood the role of a priest: to mediate between God and man; to demonstrate by word and action what God is like; to meet the physical and spiritual needs of people; and to be holy — set apart for the Lord. They recognized that God's kingdom reigned whenever his "priesthood," the community of his people, obeyed him and put his will and character on display. How would God's presence among his partners in redemption help them to be faithful to him and live as a kingdom of priests that would continually demonstrate who God is so that others would come to know him? (See Exodus 29:45 – 46; 33:12 – 17; Leviticus 26:11 – 13.)

POINT TO PONDER
How Could God "Live" on Earth?

Our finite minds can't fully understand the great paradox of a holy, transcendent God who is immanent among his people. How could the majestic God of Israel live among his people in a small tent shrine or even in a magnificent temple? How could God be Israel's Lord and King and also be her husband?

The ancient tabernacle encompassed both concepts.[5] The holy, omnipresent, unseen God was at the same time present with Israel, living in the Holy of Holies of the tabernacle between the cherubim on the ark of the covenant. His presence among his people set Israel apart from all other nations. As they demonstrated the nature of his presence living among them, God would become known to the world.

The ministry of the priest was to keep God's people continually aware of his presence among them, to instruct Israel in their daily spiritual "walk" so that they would faithfully obey him as a people and as individuals, and to demonstrate God's nature to the world.

Reflection

God has gone to great lengths to have a dwelling place among his people. At Mount Sinai, he drew his people to himself. He showed them how he would live among them and taught them what they must do to maintain his presence with them. He used fire as a visible symbol to signify his presence with them, and it had a powerful impact on his people (Exodus 19:16 – 19; 20:18 – 19; Leviticus 9:22 – 24).

Read Acts 2:1 – 4. Notice what represented the presence of God and appeared on Jesus' disciples during the Jewish feast of Pentecost. Their knowledge of what had happened at Mount Sinai made the location of God's presence clear to every Jew who witnessed that event. Take some time to study the chart below and the accompanying portions of the Text so that you can better comprehend what it means that God's presence lives in the hearts of his people.

DID YOU KNOW?
God's Presence Lives with His People

On Mount Sinai	During Pentecost
God's presence was accompanied by fire, smoke, and the sound of thunder (Exodus 19:16 – 19; 20:18 – 19).	God's presence was accompanied by a sound like wind, tongues of fire, and the gift of languages, which in Hebrew is the same word as thunder (Acts 2:1 – 4). The Hebrew term translated "Holy Spirit," *Ruach HaKodesh*, means "Holy Wind."
God's presence was symbolized by a cloud and fire, which led the Israelites out of Egypt. Later, God moved his presence into the tabernacle and the temple (Leviticus 9:22 – 24; 2 Chronicles 5:7 – 8, 13 – 14).	God's presence, evident in rushing wind and tongues of fire, moved from the temple into a new "temple" — the followers of Jesus (Romans 8:9; 1 Corinthians 3:16 – 17).
God met Moses — the Israelites' leader — on Mount Sinai, "the mountain of God" (Exodus 24:13 – 18).	Jerusalem was built on a mountain called "the mountain of the Lord" (Isaiah 2:3).

After God gave the Torah to Moses, the people worshiped the golden calf. About 3,000 people died as punishment for their sin (Exodus 32:1–4, 19–20, 27–28).	When Jesus' Spirit was given, many people repented and about 3,000 believed and found spiritual life (Acts 2:41).
The Torah (*Torah* means "teaching") provided God's teachings for his ancient community of people (Deuteronomy 6:1–9).	The Holy Spirit became the Teacher (or Advocate) of believers (John 14:26).

What does it mean to you that if you are a follower of Jesus you literally are God's "sanctuary" or dwelling place on earth — that his awesome presence dwells in you?

How important is it that ...

You allow God to make you a suitable sanctuary for his awesome presence?

You remain a suitable, holy place for him to live by faithful obedience to God's Word?

His presence within you be so apparent in every part of your life that those who are outside the Father's house come to know him?

Memorize

Then have them make a sanctuary for me, and I will dwell among them.

Exodus 25:8

Day Two | God Brings His Treasured Possession to Mount Sinai

The Very Words of God

You have declared this day that the LORD is your God and that you will walk in obedience to him, that you will keep his decrees, commands and laws — that you will listen to him. And the LORD has declared this day that you are his people, his treasured possession as he promised, and that you are to keep all his commands. He has declared that he will set you in praise, fame and honor high above all the nations he has made and that you will be a people holy to the LORD your God, as he promised.

Deuteronomy 26:17 – 19

Bible Discovery

God Prepares His People for Display

The Torah uses the designation "my people" to describe Israel throughout the story of their deliverance from Egypt and God's dramatic revelation at Mount Sinai. The covenant God made with his people at Mount Sinai is pivotal in his relationship with Israel, but their agreement with God's covenant is not the moment they became the people of God. They had been designated as "God's people" since the days of Abraham.

When the Hebrews heard God's words spoken by Moses, they bowed and worshipped the Lord because they — as God's people — believed in him as their God and the God of their ancestors (Exodus 4:29 – 31). After God delivered them from Pharaoh's army at the Reed Sea, they danced and praised God, putting their trust in him and in his servant, Moses (Exodus 14:31). As God's miraculous presence led them through the perils of the desert — before there was any revelation of the "law" — the Hebrews renewed their devotion to the God of their fathers and the covenant he had made with their ancestors.

So when the Israelites came to Mount Sinai they clearly were God's treasured possession, a community of his chosen, redeemed, believing, and worshipping people. They came not to become God's people by accepting God's covenant, but through that covenant to discover their purpose and become a people who would fulfill their responsibilities in an unbelieving world. Through the exodus and their experience at Mount Sinai, God was preparing them to live in ways that put him on display.

1. When God told his people that they were his treasured possession — that he would deliver them from Egypt and had plans for their future — he mentioned past generations. What would God's people have realized about their God and their relationship with him through these messages? (See Exodus 3:15 – 18; 6:7 – 9; 19:3 – 6.)

2. The covenants God made in the past continued through the descendants of those people: God would keep his covenant to the descendants and the descendants were to faithfully fulfill the mission God gave to their ancestors. What were these covenants, and what mission did God ask his people to fulfill? (See Genesis 1:26 – 28; 9:1 – 17; 12:1 – 3; 15:4 – 21.)

3. The forty-day journey from Egypt to Mount Sinai was peril-
ous. At times the Hebrews were certain that they would perish. Yet each time God intervened, saving his people from
harm and sustaining them through hardship. God himself
reminded them, "I carried you on eagles' wings and brought
you to myself" (Exodus 19:4). As you read the following portions of the Text, notice how God showed his loving care for
his treasured possession, his chosen people.

The Text	How God Carried His People
Ex. 12:29–32	
Ex. 14:19–20	
Ex. 14:21–31	
Ex. 15:22–27	
Ex. 16:13–18	
Ex. 17:1–7	
Ex. 17:8–13	

DID YOU KNOW?

Imagery of the Eagle

The Israelites were at Sinai because God brought them there by his mercy,
not because of their own effort. He described his provision for them on the
journey using the beautiful metaphor of being carried on eagles' wings. Many
scholars have noted that the portrayal of God as a mother eagle is one of the
most compelling metaphors in the Hebrew Bible. In references to the eagle,
writers of the Text have noted:

- The power and length of its wings (Jeremiah 48:40; 49:22)
- The way it carries its young on its back (Deuteronomy 32:10–11)
- Its ability to soar tirelessly to great heights (Jeremiah 49:16)
- Its speed (2 Samuel 1:23; Jeremiah 4:13; Lamentations 4:19)
- Its stamina to fly great distances (Isaiah 40:31)

The Hebrews were forbidden from eating birds of prey because they were "unclean" (Leviticus 11:13), yet more than thirty times the Text depicts the eagle as a metaphor of strength, stamina, and deliverance. The eagle portrays power and speed, and, along with the lion, ox, and human, appears as one of the four faces of the cherubim that surround the Lord's throne in heaven (Ezekiel 1:10–14; Revelation 4:7). The speed and power of God's deliverance of Israel is prominent in the exodus account.

It is believed that mother eagles train their young to fly by pushing them out of the nest so that they can try their wings. Because the young flounder and are in danger, the eagle then swoops beneath them, catching them and carrying them to safety with her own strong wings.

When the time was right, God nudged the Israelites out of the "nest" that was Egypt. In the wilderness they were helpless and vulnerable. When they faltered from no water, no bread, and attack by enemies, he swooped down and carried them.

Slowly but surely, while protecting them in the shelter of his "wings," he taught them how to fly—to take on responsibility for their role as his witnesses in a broken world.

4. God didn't just swoop in and save his chosen people because of his compassion; he was training them to "fly" as his partners in accomplishing his mission.

   a. What difference in maturity do you notice between how the Hebrews responded to the situation at the Reed (Red) Sea and, less than forty days later, when they faced the Amalekites? (See Exodus 14:10–14; 17:8–13.)

b. Now consider the difference in the Hebrews' faith
between Exodus 14:10 - 14, 31 and Joshua 3:9 - 17; 4:18 - 24
forty years later. Although it was always God's strength
that enabled them to carry out his purposes, what were
his people learning?

Reflection

It can be intimidating for us to consider our responsibility as partners in God's mission to restore *shalom* to his world. The task is so
big; the dangers frighten us; we feel so inadequate. But God is merciful and kind, swift and powerful to act on behalf of his children
who cry out for his help.

What has been your experience in going through a difficult time
and later realizing that God had sustained you every moment?

When has God "carried" you — or someone you love — through
a challenging situation, and what happened in your relationship
with God as a result?

It's a paradox that God asks us to give everything we have to fulfill
his mission — to "love the LORD your God with all your heart and
with all your soul and with all your strength" (Deuteronomy 6:5)
and "live as Jesus did" (1 John 2:6) — yet everything we have is the
result of the strength of his "wings." God will do amazing things for
those who are willing to be his redemptive partners (Deuteronomy

4:32 – 39). He will forgive when we fall short, lead us through difficult circumstances, deliver us by his mighty hand, and discipline us — all to prepare us to take on a greater role in his mission of redemption.

> In what ways does your view of the challenges you face change when you realize that God does the "heavy lifting" to carry us through those difficulties as he prepares us to be his partners in redemption?

Day Three | God Calls a Kingdom of Priests

The Very Words of God

> *Now if you obey me fully and keep my covenant, then out of all nations you will be my treasured possession. Although the whole earth is mine, you will be for me a kingdom of priests and a holy nation.*
>
> **Exodus 19:5 – 6**

Bible Discovery

God Wants His People to Serve Him as a Kingdom of Priests

God's redemption of the ancient Hebrew people was based on his grace and mercy, not because of anything they had done for him. *God* chose them to be his people. *God* delivered them from bondage. *God* carried them safely to himself at his mountain. In response to all that he had done for Israel, God proposed a "therefore." He asked his people for a commitment of faith to honor their covenant by their obedience in carrying out his mission.

In the few words of Exodus 19:5 – 6, God outlines the unique relationship he desires with his people, their obligations in that relationship, and the mission to which he calls them: "Now if you obey me fully and keep my covenant, then out of all nations you will be my treasured possession. Although the whole earth is mine, you will be for me a kingdom of priests and a holy nation."

In the ancient world priests served countless pagan gods, so their role was well known in the culture. The Israelites would recognize that as God's kingdom of priests they were called to mediate between God and people, show by word and action what God is like, meet human needs (spiritual as well as physical), and be holy or set apart to serve their God. Their mission was to be God's witness in every activity of life. They were to be his light to the nations (Isaiah 42:6 – 7) and make his name — his character, his reputation — known to all the world.

We, however, don't share the same cultural experiences as the ancient Hebrews. We don't have as clear a picture of what God intends when he calls his redeemed people to be his kingdom of priests. To better understand that mission, let's explore the roles and responsibilities of Israel's priests. Let's see what we can discover about being God's kingdom of priests to all nations.

1. The Hebrew word *cohen*, which is translated "priest" in Exodus 28:1, literally means "to serve." It seems *cohen* is related to the Hebrew word *kivun*, which means "to direct or show." So a priest serves God and shows others how to do the same. Above all else, who were God's priests to serve? (See Exodus 28:1 – 4.)

2. God does not intend for his partners in redemption to simply deliver a verbal message. Rather, he wants a people who are willing to *be* his message — a visual, tangible display of God. This is why, when commissioning Moses to speak to Pharaoh (Exodus 7:1), God said, "I have made you like God to Pharaoh." God wants a people who, by walking faithfully with him, experience him in such an intimate and powerful way that those who do not know God can't help but be drawn to him.

a.   As you read the following passages, take note of how the nations came to know God by observing his people and their relationship with him. (See Leviticus 26:45; Deuteronomy 4:5 – 8; 28:9 – 10; 1 Chronicles 16:8 – 10; Psalm 67; Isaiah 12:4; 61:8 – 9; Ezekiel 39:7.)

b.   What do you realize about how God's reign would grow as his people obeyed him by being his message to their world?

DID YOU KNOW?

Israel's Priests: Making God and His Laws Known

Being set apart as a priest of Israel was a great privilege and responsibility. God gave specific instructions for everything the priests who served him in the tabernacle were to do. There was no uncertainty that they were representing the God of Israel by their service. Even the clothing they wore when serving in

THE HIGH PRIEST, SERVING GOD IN THE TABERNACLE

the sanctuary reflected their high calling as servants of God's kingdom. The color blue was prominent particularly on the ephod—an apron or vest worn during tabernacle service. This artist's rendering is likely what it looked like, although no one can know exactly. The blue fabric was made with a dye produced from a small snail found along the Mediterranean Sea coast and was extremely expensive. Due to its great value, blue was associated with royalty and religious dress.

3. The responsibilities of Israel's priests included making God and his laws known to the people. They did this by teaching and reminding the people of God's presence as they ministered before God in the tabernacle. Rabbi Jonathan Sacks[6] describes the priest as one who "takes the fire of God, the high drama of sacrificial love, and the awe of the divine Presence — life-changing experiences — and turns them into daily rituals so that they become not rare and exceptional events but routines that shape the character of a nation, forming the text and texture of its collective life."

    a. In what ways did the work of the priests help God's people remember that he lived among them, and why is that essential to God's mission? (See Exodus 29:38 – 46; 40:33 – 38; Leviticus 26:11 – 13.)

    b. Israel's priests did not teach by "handing out the curriculum and giving a test." They wanted people to know and experience God's Word. Read the following passages and note how the priests not only taught God's Word but obeyed, administered, preserved, and put the Word into practice every day. How would teaching by both word and example through the events of daily life help God's people learn how to carry out his mission? (See 2 Chronicles 15:3; 19:8 – 9; Ezra 7:11 – 13; Nehemiah 8:1 – 6; Jeremiah 18:18; Malachi 2:4 – 7.)

4. God was intimately involved in teaching his people. Deuteronomy 4:35 says, "You were shown these things so that you might know that the LORD is God." That privilege of discovering who God is came with the responsibility to use their experience and knowledge to make God known to others.

    a. Notice how some of God's faithful servants carried out their responsibility to make God known. (See Exodus 8:8 – 11; Joshua 4:23 – 24; 1 Samuel 17:45 – 47; 1 Kings 8:56 – 61; 18:36 – 39; 2 Kings 19:17 – 19.)

    b. It is an amazing privilege for ordinary people who accept God's calling as priests to bear such influential witness of his revelation that those who do not know him "get it" and choose to honor him! In each of the situations below, what have those who do not follow God come to realize — or what will they realize — about him through the words and actions of God's kingdom of priests? (See Ezra 1:1 – 3; Psalm 67:1 – 5; Isaiah 2:1 – 5; Daniel 2:46 – 48; 3:28 – 30; 4:37; 6:16 – 27; Zechariah 8:20 – 23.)

5. As stated in the following passages, what did God want his kingdom of priests to be and do for the pagan people among whom they lived?

Isaiah 42:6 - 7; 51:4 - 6; 60:1 - 3

Exodus 10:16 - 19; Isaiah 56:3 - 8; Jeremiah 29:4 - 7

Reflection

There is yet another privilege and responsibility for those who would serve God as his kingdom of priests, and Israel was uniquely prepared to fill this role. As God trained Israel to display him to their world, he reminded them repeatedly of their time in Egypt when they were brutally oppressed and cried out to God because of their suffering. He heard their *ze'akah* — the desperate, pained cry of those who are helpless and hopeless — and he delivered them with his mighty hand. He restored them to the provision, protection, and relationship of his *beth ab*. So he commands his redeemed people also to tune their ears and respond to the *ze'akah* of the world around them.

How important is it to God that his people display his compassion, care, protection, and provision for those who are marginalized and in need? (See Exodus 22:21 - 24; Leviticus 19:9 - 10, 14, 32 - 34; 23:22; Deuteronomy 24:17 - 22.)

To what extent do you see God's people today being his kingdom of priests by displaying his character and love to the marginalized?

How motivated are you to be more faithful in this regard?

It is good to minister to the physical needs of those who suffer, but there is more to it than that for God's kingdom of priests. When God hears a *ze'akah,* he hears the cry of a soul that is outside the *beth ab.* If we want to be God's partners in restoring the *shalom* of his kingdom to a broken world, we must hear that cry as well. We attend to the needs of those who suffer not just to relieve their pain; we serve to show who God is so that those who are lost will come to know him as their Redeemer who welcomes them into the protection and provision of his *beth ab.*

How can you be more faithful in displaying God's heart for restoring his lost children to himself?

Memorize

Live such good lives among the pagans that, though they accuse you of doing wrong, they may see your good deeds and glorify God on the day he visits us.

1 Peter 2:12

Day Four | Chosen and Saved to Be Holy to the Lord

The Very Words of God

> *You have declared this day that the* LORD *is your God and that you will
> walk in obedience to him, that you will keep his decrees, commands
> and laws — that you will listen to him. And the* LORD *has declared this
> day that you are his people, his treasured possession as he promised,
> and that you are to keep all his commands. He has declared that he will
> set you in praise, fame and honor high above all the nations he has
> made and that you will be a people holy to the* LORD *your God, as he
> promised.*
>
> Deuteronomy 26:17 – 19

Bible Discovery

Set Apart by Obedience

Obedience is the appropriate response of a grateful heart to God's
redeeming grace. God chose Israel to be his bride, redeemed her,
and called her to a life of obedience — not so that the Hebrews
could *become* his people, but because they *were* his people. His call
to obedience gave them a way to express their love for him and to
enjoy the fullness of their relationship with him. They were to be
a redeemed people who walked in his righteousness, heeded his
voice, and at every time and in every place carried out the mission
he had entrusted to them.

The obedience God required would also set them apart as a distinct witness to him. He commanded them to be holy (Hebrew:
kadosh, "set apart") as he is holy, to have priorities and practices
that differed from those of their pagan neighbors. By obeying God's
commands, Israel would imitate God, "so that when others see that
faithful lifestyle they catch a glimpse of the nature of God."[7]

Obedience to God isn't an easy path to walk in the world. Israel was
tempted to be like the surrounding nations and to ignore the commands of the God who redeemed and commissioned them. Their
unfaithfulness grieved God — in part because they were no longer

displaying him to his lost children. At other times, Israel tended to be so "set apart" that they had no interaction with people who needed to discover Israel's God through their righteous living. Let's see what God did to give them an ever-present reminder of their redemption and holy calling as his kingdom of priests.

1. After they committed themselves to God's reign in their lives, God commissioned Israel to be his "kingdom of priests" in the world. What did he provide for them so they would know how to obey him in every part of their lives? (See Exodus 24:12.)

2. As the story of the exodus unfolds in the Text, notice the key things that God brings to the attention of his people. Which phrase does God use repeatedly and why do you think it is so important for his people to grasp it? (See Exodus 20:1 – 6; Deuteronomy 4:35 – 40; 6:20 – 24; 7:7 – 11; 11:7 – 8.)

3. What command did God give to Israel that would set his people apart from the world around them and continually remind them to faithfully obey their calling as God's kingdom of priests to all nations? (See Numbers 15:37 – 41; Deuteronomy 22:12.)

FOR GREATER UNDERSTANDING

Clothing Sends a Message

In ancient times, the clothing people wore often revealed their identity and societal status. The hem and tassels (or fringe; Hebrew: *tzitzit*) of the outer robe were particularly important, symbolizing the owner's identity and authority. So significant was the hem that a corner of it was sometimes pressed into clay to leave an impression as the owner's official seal. Those in the upper class—nobility, kings, and princes—decorated their hems with tassels.

God wanted his people to stand out as unique among the nations—morally, socially, economically, and religiously—because of their obedience to him. He also commanded them to make tassels and wear them on the corners of their clothing, ensuring that they would never be anonymous in public.[8] Even at a distance, their distinctive clothing declared that the Most High God had chosen them out of all others to be his kingdom of priests and that they had chosen

A FATHER EXPLAINS THE TASSELS.

to obey him. In a sense, God's command to wear tassels gave them a uniform that identified them as his own.[9]

By wearing tassels, the Hebrews wore what appeared to be robes of royalty—a reminder to both Jews and Gentiles of their status as God's holy, chosen people. The tassels were a statement of their identity as God's kingdom of priests who in every activity of life were to display God to the world and show how he wanted people to live. The tassels also were a constant reminder to obey God's commands—always. If they failed to obey, they would be hypocrites and would portray a flawed picture of the God who chose them to be his partners in redemption.

4. The tassels are also one way God's mission is passed from generation to generation. According to one Jewish saying, "The most important question is not 'Did you have faithful parents?' but rather 'Will you have faithful grandchildren?'" Read Deuteronomy 6:1 – 2, 4 – 9 and imagine a Jewish parent obeying this command by teaching a child how to wear tassels or explaining why God gave this command and why obedience is important. How could a person go about teaching the importance of loving God and faithfully living out his mission without using tassels?

Reflection

Israel was commanded to be holy as God is holy. They were set apart for the unique purpose of imitating God in all that they did so that all people would come to know who God is. Yet holiness doesn't happen just because we have been forgiven and redeemed. Holiness is a task, a quality we acquire as we learn to imitate God in all of life. The commandments God gave to his people at Mount Sinai showed how to imitate him!

Take time to read through the commandments God gave in Leviticus 19. Based on what you read, make a list of what God said holiness should look like in the lives of his people. (You should have a dozen or more descriptions.)

Then consider the world in which you live. Specifically identify how to obey these commandments in your life, describing what holiness that displays God accurately would look like.

Finally, ask yourself if you are living in such a way as to put God on display in everything you do, every minute of every day, or if you are trying to be anonymous and hope that no one notices.

Memorize

The LORD will establish you as his holy people, as he promised you on oath, if you keep the commands of the LORD your God and walk in obedience to him. Then all the peoples on earth will see that you are called by the name of the LORD, and they will fear you.

Deuteronomy 28:9 – 10

Day Five | Living the Great Commission Today

The Very Words of God

But you are a chosen people, a royal priesthood, a holy nation, God's special possession, that you may declare the praises of him who called you out of darkness into his wonderful light. Once you were not a people, but now you are the people of God; once you had not received mercy, but now you have received mercy.

1 Peter 2:9 – 10

Bible Discovery

God's Kingdom Comes as His People Make Him Known

At Sinai, God gave his redeemed people the great commission to extend his reign over every dimension of life — to further his kingdom by obeying him as Lord so that all people would experience his blessing. People who have made a faith commitment to Jesus also have been saved by God's grace through Jesus' redeeming sacrifice. Just as God's redemption of Israel led to a "therefore," the redemption of those who follow Jesus leads to a "therefore."

God saves us and then commissions us, as his royal priesthood, to a task that encompasses all of life. He calls us to a life of obedience to his commands so that we can be witnesses of his message. He calls us to live in such a way that we extend the reign of his kingdom in our fractured world.

As his redeemed people, we are God's witnesses — the Word in flesh. We are his priests who do his will so that his kingdom will come. Will we respond to his commission in faithful obedience — enabled by his Spirit, guided by his Text, supported by his community — and be his witnesses through our every action and word to those who do not yet know God?

1. God met his redeemed people on Mount Sinai, gave them a commission to extend his reign in every dimension of life, and showed them how to express their love for him. What similarities do you see in what Jesus taught those who would follow him about extending his reign and showing their love for him? (See Matthew 6:33; 7:21 - 22; 8:11; 12:46 - 50; Luke 6:46 - 49; John 14:15, 23 - 24; 1 John 2:1 - 6; 5:3; 2 John 1:6.)

    a. What is the mission of those who claim Jesus as Lord, and how important is it to him? (See John 14:15, 23 - 24; 2 Timothy 1:8 - 12; Titus 2:11 - 14.)

b. What strong warning does Jesus have for those who do not obey him? (See Luke 6:46 – 49.)

FOR GREATER UNDERSTANDING
God's Kingdom Comes as His People Do His Will

Jesus recognized the conflict between the kingdom of heaven (God) and the kingdom of the Evil One. He declared (Luke 11:14 – 20) that if the "finger of God" defeats the power of evil, then God's kingdom has come. His biblically literate audience no doubt understood that Jesus was pointing to the kingdom God announced at Mount Sinai — that they were his kingdom of priests if they fully obeyed the word of the Lord and kept his covenant.

Many people who saw God's power evidenced in Jesus' healing and teaching called him *Lord* (Matthew 8:2, 8) as their ancestors had at the Reed (Red) Sea. As important as that faith commitment was, it was not enough. God redeemed his people by his powerful grace and expected them to then submit to his reign by obeying his words. Through their obedience, they put their faith into practice and became a kingdom of priests. Jesus also invited people to put their faith in him, to call him Savior and Lord, and then to make him their King by doing his will so that his reign would be extended.

2. Read Exodus 19:3 - 6, then 1 Peter 2:4 - 12.

    a. What is God still doing to extend his kingdom and restore *shalom* to a broken world?

    b. As God's treasured possession, set apart to display him to our broken world, how are we to represent God, to express his love and concern to all nations?

    c. If God's kingdom of priests does its job, what will be the result?

3. Jesus came to redeem all of humanity, and by his example of obedience to the Father he also showed us what the kingdom of God looks like. What do you learn about being a priest of God's kingdom from Jesus' example?

The Text	What a Priest of God's Kingdom Looks Like
Heb. 7:24 - 28	
Matt. 20:28; Luke 22:26 - 27	
John 1:14; 14:9 - 11	
Luke 24:50 - 53[10]	

Heb. 4:15–16	
Matt. 8:18–19; 12:38; John 13:12–17	
Mark 10:21; Luke 4:18; 14:13–14	
Matt. 26:63–64; Luke 22:70; John 7:28–29	

Reflection

God brought Israel to Sinai to commission them to be his "partner," a holy kingdom of priests influencing the whole world through example and word that their God was Lord and Savior. He called his people to holiness, not only for their sake but for the sake of the nations that would see them and thereby come to know him and his ways. Those of us who are God's people today must also engage our broken world — not as power brokers forcing change on others but as those who display the presence of Jesus — the kingdom of God — in everything we do. The world needs us ... No, the world needs God! And he still chooses to make his presence known in and through his people — his royal priesthood.

A lecture from Chief Rabbi Lord Jonathan Sacks to a Jewish audience also speaks powerfully to Jesus followers who accept God's call to join with his royal priesthood and display him to our world.[11] In summary, he offers three options for those who would be his witnesses to our world:

1. We can assimilate and be like the broken world we are called to affect. Our lifestyles can be dominated by the pursuit of pleasure, leisure, and material wealth. Our attitudes and actions concerning wealth can be shaped by a culture that connects happiness with possessions and meaning by how much we earn or own. Our sexual values and mores can be

shaped by the media, what the majority believes, or what feels good. When we allow our culture to shape us, we give up our role and influence as God's kingdom of priests.

2. We can isolate, living in safe communities and limiting our contact with those who have differing values. We can attempt to protect our lives and possessions with little regard for the suffering of others. This choice, also, is dangerous. If we have little to do with the world, we fail to understand it and leave ourselves [and our children] defenseless against it.

3. We can engage. Sacks writes, "The world needs the Jews and Jews need the world."[12] I would paraphrase: "The world needs Christians and Christians need the world." When God's people engage our world in a creative, positive, and compassionate way, we enhance the lives of others — particularly those who suffer. We also bring honor to God's name and draw others to him. We have been called to be God's priests to a dying world. What if we came with the life-giving words and actions of the God who loves all his children and wants to restore them to his family? Again in Rabbi Sacks' words, in a challenge to Jewish people (and I would say, to Jesus followers as well):

    > What if Jews [and Jesus followers] would be found disproportionately as doctors fighting disease, lawyers fighting injustice, educators fighting ignorance, economists fighting poverty, etc.[13] ... Imagine a Judaism [and a Christianity] that engaged our greatest minds, our top professionals, our leading business people, our most creative artists, musicians and film producers, encouraging them to go out into the world making a contribution as role models and exemplars of faith — the faith in God that leads us to have faith in the possibility of defeating the reign of violence, terror, injustice and oppression? ... We are bearers of the Divine presence, witness in ourselves to something far greater than ourselves, living proof of the dignity of difference and of the power of faith to heal a fractured world.[14]

If we love God, we must obey him and learn how to be his kingdom of priests in our world. As his partner in redeeming a world in chaos, read the following verses and prayerfully consider how you will:

Mediate between God and people through the Holy Spirit within you. (See Acts 2:1 - 12; 1 Corinthians 3:16 - 17; Ephesians 2:19 - 22.)

I will: _____

Demonstrate by word and action what God is like. (See Matthew 5:14 - 16, 38 - 47; 6:9; 28:19 - 20; John 17:20 - 23; 1 Corinthians 11:1; James 1:19 - 21, 26; 1 Peter 2:11 - 12.)

I will: _____

Meet human needs in God's name. (See Matthew 25:31 - 46; 2 Corinthians 9:6 - 11; James 1:22 - 27; 5:14 - 16.)

I will: _____

Be holy. (See Romans 12:1 - 2, 9 - 21; Ephesians 5:1 - 11; Colossians 3:12 - 14.)

I will: _____

JESUS RENEWS THE MISSION: SEEKING THE LOST

God created the heavens and the earth and entrusted his creation to the care of the humans he formed. But they proved to be unfaithful partners. Their rebellion and sin shattered God's beautiful handiwork. How would he restore his creation to its original perfection? By his grace, he again invited human partners to join him in the mission of redeeming his creation.

God chose Abraham and Sarah (by covenant, their descendants as well) to be his partners in the mission of redemption and to be his instruments of blessing to all nations. When the time came, God redeemed their descendants — the Israelites — from slavery in Egypt. He brought them to Mount Sinai and commissioned them to be his kingdom of priests, a holy nation that would display him to a world that did not know him. Through the words and actions of God's obedient people, his name — his character, his reputation — would be made known. Israel would be a light to the Gentiles so that all nations would experience God's restoration. That was, and still is, the mission God entrusts to his people.

God knew the task would not be easy. His chosen partners would have to be faithful to his covenant with them, obeying all of his commands so that their witness would accurately portray him. So God loved them, taught them, and lavished his resources on them. He provided for them in the wilderness. Through the tabernacle he established a place and practices so that he could live with them. And he instructed them to wear tassels on their robes as a constant reminder to obey every word that came from his mouth.

Even so, God's chosen people struggled with their mission. Sometimes they were holy and lived faithfully, but often they were unfaithful. They forgot the meaning of their tassels with the blue cord that reminded them that they were set apart to be a kingdom of priests. As time passed, they assimilated pagan practices and lived as if God's abundant blessings were for their own benefit rather than a means of sharing God's blessing with others. God disciplined them through suffering, oppression, and eventually allowed them to be taken to a foreign land.

The time in captivity got their attention. When they returned to the Promised Land, God's people renewed their commitment to be holy — to always remember the blue cord and obey God's commands. Sometimes, however, their zeal was so strong that they forgot the purpose of their holiness. It was not to make them acceptable to God — that came by his grace. It was to witness to unrighteous nations that God loved them, too.

Then Jesus came to earth and lived among God's people. His central focus was redeeming God's broken world by paying the penalty for human sin through his death and resurrection. And he also came to be an example of how to carry out God's mission. By his obedient, holy life he stood apart as a living testimony of God to Jew and Gentile alike. He was a light to the nations, honoring the name of God and making him known to all.

As God's partner in redemption, Jesus called Israel back to faithfulness to the mission God gave on Mount Sinai. When the Jews chose unrighteousness over holiness, he called them to repentance and obedience by word and example. When their commitment to righteousness overrode their mission to reach out to "sinners," he demanded by word and action that they seek the spiritually lost in order to bring them back into relationship with the Father. Jesus also renewed the commission God gave Israel at Mount Sinai, adding new content to the original mission: to bless all nations through Abraham's physical descendants and Gentiles who were adopted into his family through the Messiah.

This study focuses on Jesus' renewal of Israel's mission and its implications for his followers. When he was criticized for having close contact with sinners (and by implication, no longer being holy),

Jesus countered with a three-part parable that dramatically portrayed God's intense love for lost sinners. The parable also invited his hearers to accept their role as God's partners in the mission of seeking sinners so that they may be restored to the Father's house. Based on the foundation of God's commission to Israel to be his kingdom of priests, this parable calls us, as Jesus' followers who also are commissioned to be his royal priesthood, to greater faithfulness in seeking the lost and displaying God's redemptive love. We, like Israel, are to be "seekers of the lost" joining God's ancient story in which all nations will be blessed by being restored to the God who loves them.

Opening Thoughts (3 minutes)

The Very Words of God

> Jesus said to him, "Today salvation has come to this house, because this man, too, is a son of Abraham. For the Son of Man came to seek and to save the lost."
>
> *Luke 19:9–10*

Think About It

As followers of Jesus today, we may feel comfortable inviting people who are spiritually "lost" to join us in church or to participate in special events that teach about God's love and redemption. Jesus, on the other hand, accepted invitations to fellowship with those who were lost — eating with sinners, as his critics pointed out.

How far out of our "comfort zone" are we willing to go to seek out those in our world who are spiritually lost?

What criticism might we face from others in our faith community if we, in a genuine effort to make God known, truly engaged with people who do not know him — sinners — where they live, work, and play?

DVD Notes (29 minutes)

A land of sheep and shepherds

The resources of the father's house

Life in the father's house

A three-part parable about finding what is lost
Rejoice! The shepherd finds his lost sheep

Rejoice! The woman finds her lost coin

A lost son turns his back on the father's house

DVD Discussion (9 minutes)

1. This study was filmed in the restored Talmudic village of
    Qatzrin, a fascinating archaeological site near Galilee, the
    region where Jesus did much of his teaching. Although the
    ruins at this site are dated about three centuries after the
    time of Jesus, the building design, construction methods,
    and cultural practices changed little during that time.[1] So this
    location is helpful for understanding the setting and lifestyle
    of the people Jesus lived among and for gaining insight into
    his teaching. What insights did you gain regarding how tightly
    connected such a community would be — how well people
    would know each other, the close-knit relationships of an
    extended family living together in one house, and how diffi-
    cult it would be to be viewed as an outcast in this community?

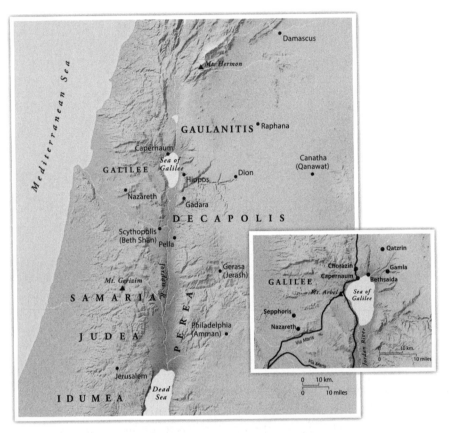

On your map, locate Qatzrin, Gamla, Capernaum, Bethsaida, and Jerash. Notice how close the Decapolis was to the villages of Galilee — sometimes just across the Sea of Galilee or over a distant hill! One can see this "far country" from the village of Capernaum where Jesus lived during his teaching ministry.

2. God gave Israel his presence in the tabernacle, his words in the Torah, his promise to provide for them, and examples of godly people who obeyed his commands as resources to help them restore his lost children to his *beth ab*. Give some thought to God's intended purpose for the resources he has provided *you*.

   a. To what extent have you assumed that God's provision was for your benefit rather than for the purpose of restoring those who are lost to his *beth ab*?

b. What resources has God given to you for the restoration of his lost sheep, and how might you make better use of them?

3. As you consider the parables Jesus told, as well as his own example, what did you hear about the level of concern, commitment, and effort required to seek and to find that which is lost?

4. Notice that in each parable Jesus included a celebration of the effort expended to seek and restore the lost sheep, coin, and son. How do you think those who criticized Jesus felt about him eating with sinners and celebrating not only that they had been found but that he was the one who had found them?

5. What kind of stir do you think this interaction between Jesus and the Pharisees and teachers of the law created in a community that was much like Qatzrin? What might people in the community — family patriarchs, students in the synagogue school, tax collectors, Pharisees, women preparing a meal together — have talked about amongst themselves in response to what they heard?

FOR GREATER UNDERSTANDING
Life in a Galilean Village

In the excavated and reconstructed village of Qatzrin, we find family homes, sometimes called *insulae* (*insula*, singular), in which several generations of an extended family lived together. Each family home was known as "the father's house" and included as many as fifteen rooms built around a large, open courtyard. The courtyard likely had a partial roof and functioned as the main living space because the mild Mediterranean climate made it possible to work and eat outside.

Inside, each home also had a large multi-purpose room, called a *traqlin,* a small kitchen with a clay oven, storage or workrooms, and an upper loft. The *traqlin* most likely had benches along the outside walls and probably mats on the basalt cobblestone floor. The family entertained guests, ate meals, and performed household tasks during colder winter months here. When Jesus described activities in a typical home or ate in someone's house, they likely occurred in the

A TYPICAL COURTYARD

A TRAQLIN, OR MULTIPURPOSE ROOM

traqlin. Rooms adjacent to the *traqlin* were separated by a wall in which there were a series of windows and an entrance that allowed passage from one room into another. The window wall, which provided support for the ceiling and second story above, also allowed light and ventilation.

As the family grew, rooms were added to meet the family's additional needs. When a son married, the patriarch oversaw the addition of a new room—the wedding chamber. The Talmud records that the building of the chamber for a son was cause for great joy![2] After several generations of additions, the family complex would include many connected household units.

Although they date two centuries after Jesus lived in Capernaum a few miles away, the extended family homes in Qatzrin are typical of the homes in which Jesus lived and taught. They also represent the setting for some of his parables, such as the lost coin and the prodigal son. All of the villages where Jesus taught in Galilee were constructed of the same black, volcanic stone.

Small Group Bible Discovery and Discussion (14 minutes)

Redemption from God's Perspective

In the world of the Bible, the concept of redemption was rooted in cultural rather than religious practice. Life in the ancient Middle East revolved around the extended family, and a person's connection to society came through the family. The patriarch controlled all family resources. He was responsible to protect the resources, ensure that they remained within the family, and use them for the benefit of everyone in the clan. If a member was marginalized and lost connection to the family (due to irresponsible actions, oppression, poverty, circumstances beyond his control, etc.), the patriarch was responsible to redeem that person. He would seek and find the lost one, rescue the lost one from trouble, and pay whatever price was necessary to restore that person fully to the "father's house." The term *ga'al* meant "redeem" and described that restoration.

The inspired writers of the Text chose redemption as a metaphor to describe God's plan to restore *shalom* to his creation and bring his lost children back into relationship with him. He is portrayed as the loving Father, intent on seeking out and redeeming his lost family.[3] Christians commonly use the word *gospel,* meaning "good news," to summarize the redemptive message of the Bible, particularly the New Testament message of God sending his only Son to die so that sinners might place their faith in him, be forgiven, and receive eternal life. Notice how John 3:16 summarizes the good news within the metaphor of God as Redeemer: "For God [as patriarch] so loved the world [his lost family members] that he gave his one and only Son [paid whatever price necessary], that whoever believes in him shall not perish but have eternal life [be restored to his *beth ab*]."

1. The following verses give us a picture of our loving Father's efforts to redeem his lost children and restore them fully to his family. What do each of the following verses add to your understanding of God as Redeemer? (See Exodus 15:13; Isaiah 43:1; Luke 1:68–75; Ephesians 1:7; 1 Peter 1:18–19.)

2. To "redeem" means that a patriarch would seek and find the lost, rescue the lost from whatever trouble they were in, and restore the lost fully to the community of the *beth ab*. God did this for his people when he brought them out of Egypt. Read Exodus 6:6–8, Deuteronomy 7:8–9, and 1 Chronicles 17:20–22.

    a. Why did God seek out his people when they were in Egypt?

    b. What trouble or bondage were they in?

    c. What was required to secure their redemption?

d. How were they restored to relationship with the Father?

3. Spiritual restoration, or *salvation* as we often call it, is the foundation of God's redemption and restoration of his lost children. In the New Testament context, redemption focuses more specifically on the spiritual than the physical or material, yet the elements of redemption remain the same.

a. Why does God seek out his lost children? (See 1 John 4:10.)

b. What is the spiritual bondage from which we need to be delivered? (See John 8:34 – 36; Romans 3:23; 6:16 – 18.)

c. What was required to secure our spiritual redemption? (See Mark 10:45; 1 Corinthians 6:20.)

d. How are we restored to relationship with the Father? (See Galatians 4:5; Colossians 1:13 – 14.)

4. God's mission for Israel was for them to become his agents of redemption in the world. They were to obey God's commands so that they would display his heart, reflect his character, and model his ways for people who did not know him. They especially were to have compassion for and seek out the marginalized so they could be brought to forgiveness and restored fully to God's household. This was Jesus' mission as well. He came to encourage Israel to return to her mission as God's partner in redemption and to proclaim a message that echoes Israel's redemption. Notice how Jesus instructs his followers to walk in the ways of the Lord as his partners in redemption:

Matthew 19:16 – 21

Matthew 20:25 – 28

John 15:12 – 17

THINK ABOUT IT
The Value of What Is Lost

Luke 15 provides an account of Jesus' teaching about redeeming that which is lost. Although we may think of this teaching as three different parables, it is actually one parable in three parts. The teaching began with "this parable," (Luke 15:3[4]) followed by "or suppose," and the last part started with "Jesus continued." As the parable progressed, the value of what is lost increases.

Sheep were valuable, providing wool and milk to sell and, on rare occasions, meat to eat. Most shepherds lived in desert regions, and a family commonly owned a few sheep. A person owning a hundred sheep was considered wealthy, but even the loss of one sheep would have been significant. No doubt Jesus' audience nodded in approval of the shepherd expending such effort to find a lost sheep.

The *coin* was worth more than a day's wages. Even today Bedouin women wear coins of significant value on chains around their neck or stitched to their clothes. These coins functioned as a "savings deposit box" in Jesus' ancient culture. If an emergency arose, that money met urgent needs. It would be a great misfortune if this woman was quite poor and lost one of her ten silver coins.

The *son* represented something of even higher value. In the first-century patriarchal culture, children — and sons in particular — were priceless to a family. The loss of a son was a great tragedy.

Faith Lesson (4 minutes)

God sent his Son, Jesus the Messiah, to pay the ultimate price in order to redeem all of his lost children and restore them to his house. Clearly each sinner has tremendous value in the eyes of God. If those of us who have been redeemed — a gift of grace from God — are to become effective agents of his redemption, we need to value sinners as he does.

1. Take a few moments to read Luke 15:1 – 24.

   a. What do you realize about God's desire to find and redeem that which is lost, and how much does his desire ignite yours?

b.　The Pharisees, who were devoted to God's command to seek righteousness, had difficulty recognizing sinners' worth and why God valued them so highly. In what ways do we sometimes devalue the worth of "sinners" — criticizing, avoiding, or even ostracizing people whose values, agendas, attitudes, and behaviors violate our ideas of righteousness?

c.　We might wonder if the Pharisees, who highly valued a sinner's repentance, were challenged enough by this parable to reconsider their unwillingness to engage "sinners" and "tax collectors."[5] The bigger question is, what does this parable challenge us to do?

d.　What do you think is the key to remaining devoted to righteousness like the Pharisees, yet to so highly value people who are lost that we actively seek ways to engage with them even if we oppose their beliefs and behaviors?

Closing (1 minute)

Read Galatians 3:14: "He redeemed us in order that the blessing given to Abraham might come to the Gentiles through Christ Jesus ..." Now pray, thanking God for redeeming us from the bondage of sin and welcoming each of us as his partners in seeking those who are still lost outside the protection and provision of his family. Ask for faithfulness in continuing the commission God gave to Israel to be his "priests" in a spiritually dark world. May we recognize the urgency to go out and seek those who are lost with the love, strength, and passion of our Savior, Jesus.

Memorize

He redeemed us in order that the blessing given to Abraham might come to the Gentiles through Christ Jesus …

Galatians 3:14

Restoring the Lost to the Father's House

In-Depth Personal Study Sessions

Day One | Seeking the Lost Wherever They Can Be Found

The Very Words of God

> *Now the tax collectors and sinners were all gathering around to hear Jesus. But the Pharisees and the teachers of the law muttered, "This man welcomes sinners and eats with them."*
>
> *Luke 15:1–2*

Bible Discovery

Intent on the Mission, Jesus Ate with Sinners

In Jesus' day, the word *sinner* of course described someone who was disobedient to God's will and had broken God's command-ments. The word was applied to those who were obviously evil in their actions as well as to prostitutes and irreligious or spiritually apathetic people. But *sinner* didn't always mean someone who had become ritually unclean or impure; it was even applied to those who violated interpretations of Torah on which there was disagree-ment! Tax collectors were considered to be some of the worst sin-ners. Many of them were dishonest and greedy. Others cooperated with Roman overlords or the Herodian dynasty that served Rome, so all tax collectors were viewed as traitors who opposed God.

Although many faithful Jews believed it was wrong to associate with "sinners," Jesus viewed them as God's lost children. He was deeply concerned for them and made it clear that he not only would eat with them but that their sin and impurity was the very reason he had come. Let's explore how Jesus chose to become involved in the lives of sinners in order to show them God's love, care, and compassion.

1. Try to imagine the scene of Luke 15 when Jesus responded to his critics by telling the parable of the lost sheep, lost coin, and lost son. (See Luke 15:1 – 2.)

    a. What kinds of people gathered around Jesus, and why do you think they were there? What do you think the size and atmosphere of the crowd may have been like?

    b. Given Jesus' mission, why is this scene what we would — or would not — have expected him to do?

    c. What was Jesus doing that caused concern among Pharisees and teachers of the law, and how did they express their displeasure?

DID YOU KNOW?

Why Was Eating with Sinners Such an Offense?

When describing Jesus' contact with sinners, Luke used the Greek word *prosdechomai*, which literally means "welcome into fellowship or community." The word implies a willingness to sit and converse with people and accept them as close friends. It is the same word Paul used to instruct the early church to accept a person as a brother or sister in the Lord (Romans 16:2; Philippians 2:29). Although there is no hint that Jesus approved of their sin, he wasn't just sitting down next to sinners; he was establishing close relationships with them so that through him they would know (experience) the Father's love.

From the perspective of his critics, the greater offense was that Jesus ate with sinners. In the Middle East, eating with someone is a "sacramental act signifying acceptance on a very deep level."[6] Jesus was engaging with — accepting and affirming — people who were considered to be unclean. His critics viewed Jesus' behavior as an endorsement of the lifestyle of the sinners. No wonder they were upset!

2. Jesus received criticism on other occasions for eating with "sinners," which was presumed to be an endorsement of their lifestyle. (See Matthew 9:9 – 13; Mark 2:13 – 17; Luke 7:36 – 50; 19:1 – 10.)

   a. Why, according to Jesus, did he come to earth? And why do you think eating with people was a good way to accomplish his purpose?

   b. What did Jesus do that showed compassion and respect for his critics as well as the "sinners" with whom he ate?

   c. Which people were redeemed and restored to the *shalom* of God's family as a result of their interaction with Jesus?

3. As part of his mission to seek the lost, Jesus also engaged in redemptive interaction with Gentiles — something unheard of among God-fearing Jews of his day. Read Mark 7:24 – 30 and Matthew 15:21 – 28. How did Jesus use the opportunity

that arose in Gentile Phoenicia to show the balance between being holy yet also being willing to engage with sinners and Gentiles in order to display God's character and share God's blessing with them?

4. In light of the fact that Jesus' love and acceptance of sinners does not imply approval or that he overlooked their sin, what did he expect lost children to do in response to God's grace offered to them? (See Luke 7:36 – 49; 15:7, 10; John 5:1 – 14; 8:1 – 11.)

Reflection

In the West, we in the Christian community have increasingly less impact on the culture around us. We may want to be faithful to the mission God has given us to influence our world, but we tend to isolate and insulate as individuals, families, and communities and become critical and harsh in our engagement with those who are lost. We remember that Jesus came to seek and save the lost, but we seem to have forgotten that he did it by becoming involved in their lives so that they could experience God's love. Jesus came for the sinners: he loved them, welcomed them, ate with them, and died for them.

There is a rabbinic saying: "The word [of God] must become flesh." If we claim to be God's witnesses — the Word in flesh — we must follow Jesus' example. To be a witness is to live in a certain way. It is as much about how we live as what we say. Enabled by his Spirit, guided by his Text, and supported by his community — God intends that we seek out his lost children, love them, accept them, and make God known to them so that they will welcome his redemption and allow him to restore *shalom* to their broken lives.

Jesus became involved in sinners' lives through genuine love, compassion, and care. He engaged with sinners, even those who were ostracized by the religious community.

> Who are the people in your world who probably feel rejected by the Christian community?

> Why is it difficult to accept them and connect with them, and what might you do to make it easier?

Just as Jesus' love drew sinners to God, we must find ways — individually and as a community — to seek out those whom the religious community ignores and show them who God is and how much he loves and cares for them.

> If you are determined, as Jesus was, to seek out the lost, how will you spend time with them, show that you accept them, and care deeply about their needs?

What resources and blessings has God given you that will lead these lost people to want to spend time with you, and how can you use these resources more effectively for the benefit of those who need to know the Father and experience his love?

Memorize

Therefore, if anyone is in Christ, the new creation has come: The old has gone, the new is here! All this is from God, who reconciled us to himself through Christ and gave us the ministry of reconciliation: that God was reconciling the world to himself in Christ, not counting people's sins against them. And he has committed to us the message of reconciliation. We are therefore Christ's ambassadors, as though God were making his appeal through us. We implore you on Christ's behalf: Be reconciled to God.

2 Corinthians 5:17–20

Day Two | Overzealous for Holiness?

The Very Words of God

While Jesus was having dinner at Matthew's house, many tax collectors and sinners came and ate with him and his disciples. When the Pharisees saw this, they asked his disciples, "Why does your teacher eat with tax collectors and sinners?" On hearing this, Jesus said, "It is not the healthy who need a doctor, but the sick. But go and learn what this means: 'I desire mercy, not sacrifice.' For I have not come to call the righteous, but sinners."

Matthew 9:10–13

Bible Discovery

Understanding the Heart of the Pharisees

When God called his people to himself at Mount Sinai, he called them to be a holy nation, his kingdom of priests to the world. They were set apart to *be* his message. Any compromise of their holiness would present a flawed image of God. So absolute obedience to God's every command was tremendously important to religious Jews of Jesus' day.

In order to obey God completely, Jewish people discussed and debated how the Torah was to be interpreted and applied in daily life. Focused discussion rooted in the Text and its interpretation was intensely passionate, as it is within the religious Jewish community today. To an observer from another culture, it may appear as if participants despise each other. But at prayer time the debaters come together like family; when prayers are over, debate resumes.

The ongoing debate between Jesus and the Pharisees recorded in the Gospels was an expression of this practice, as were the sharp denunciations of one's "opponents" and their points of view. Certainly Jesus disagreed with Pharisees sometimes, but he did so in a "family" setting—Jew criticizing Jew about how best to obey God. Jesus also said positive things about Pharisees and encouraged them to grow deeper in their faith. A greater understanding of the Pharisees will add insight into our study of Jesus' teaching about seeking the lost.

PROFILE OF A PEOPLE

Who Were the Pharisees?

Although God's prophets called them back to obedience many times, Israel refused to heed the call to be holy to the Lord. God could no longer tolerate its evil, so in 586 BC he allowed Nebuchadnezzar to conquer Judea and Jerusalem; the temple was destroyed, tens of thousands were killed, and survivors were taken to Babylon as slaves.

Although the temple sacrifices stopped and the priesthood no longer functioned as the Torah commanded, the Jewish exiles dedicated themselves to the study of the Text, including its interpretation and required obedience. They had a renewed passion to be God's holy people and were determined to be faithful so that he would not have to discipline them again. After seventy years, they started to return to the Promised Land. They rebuilt the temple and resumed the rituals, but for many the Torah now played a central role in everyday Jewish life.[7]

A significant lay movement focused on study of the Torah, and the people in this movement, mostly farmers, took the name *Hasid (Hasidim,* pl.), meaning "pious one." During the second century before Jesus, Seleucid Greeks — successors of Alexander the Great who had conquered Israel a century earlier and exalted human beings as supreme — severely persecuted Jews in the Promised Land and outlawed study of the Torah. Supported by the *Hasidim,* some of the bravest and mightiest warriors in recorded history, the Jewish Maccabees fought against the Greeks and triumphed in 167 BC.

However, the Maccabees' successors, known by the family name Hasmonaean, soon became as Hellenized as the Greeks. This presented a problem for the intensely devout *Hasidim.* Some continued a violent fight against the influences of paganism and Hellenism whether they appeared in Greeks, Romans, or their fellow Jews. They became known as Zealots. Others rejected violence, believing that foreign oppression was due to their lack of obedience to the Torah. These Torah teachers and scholars were devoted to God and complete obedience to every detail of his law. They became known as "the separatists" (Hebrew, *P'rushim;* English, "Pharisees") because of their intense commitment to remain separate from pagan practices and Hellenistic attitudes and to call Israel to obedience to the Torah.

The Pharisees highly valued the *Tanakh*[8] (Hebrew for what we know as the Old Testament, including the Torah), believing it was God's revelation to all people and to be accepted without question. Their life centered on the Torah, including the additional oral commandments (laws) that were passed through generations to help the faithful understand and apply the written law. As the Pharisees continued to interpret and expand the Torah to cover every possible occurrence of unfaithfulness, the oral law became a complex guide to everyday life — often beyond the comprehension of the people it was intended to help. Jesus often criticized the oral law, although he kept it in many respects.

Although the Sadducees administered temple rituals and were the ruling religious body in Jesus' day, the Pharisees were popular with ordinary people and wielded the most influence. Masters of the Torah, they were highly respected for their knowledge and expertise in the Scriptures—studying, interpreting, teaching, and modeling obedience to the Torah and the collection of oral interpretations. They were passionate about being set apart in the world to live holy lives as God had commanded.

1. Although we may view *Pharisee* as being synonymous with the hypocrisy of those Jesus criticized for understanding Scripture correctly but not practicing it faithfully, we must remember that most Pharisees were extremely devoted to God. "Eating with sinners" was not a petty judgment on their part; it deeply troubled them because of their passion for holiness and faithfulness to God in everything. Read the following verses and take note of what the Pharisees valued and were doing right.

The Text	What the Pharisees Valued and Did
Matt. 5:20	
Matt. 23:1–7	
Luke 7:36; 14:1	
Luke 13:31	
John 3:1–2	
Acts 5:34–39	
Acts 15:5	
Acts 23:6–9	

FOR GREATER UNDERSTANDING

The Synagogue in Qatzrin

The well-preserved fourth-century synagogue at Qatzrin has the typical basilica appearance of those from Jesus' time. It is similar to the village synagogues where Jesus lived and taught. The benches around the outside are known as "chief seats" and were reserved for the wise or righteous in the community. A platform on the southern end may have held a "closet" for the scrolls of the *Tanakh*. A small room on the east side was likely the school where children of this community were taught.

By Jesus' time, more than six thousand Pharisees had become a dominant influence on the spiritual lives of God's people. Because their lives revolved around study of the Torah, Pharisees made the synagogue their community center. It was likely the prominent building in the village, which demonstrates the deep commitment Jewish people had for knowing and keeping Torah. Their devotion made it possible for Jesus to teach by hinting at Bible passages that his audiences knew well. His parable about the lost sheep is an example, based on the Hebrew Bible's teaching about God being the shepherd who seeks his lost sheep.

THE SYNAGOGUE AT QATZRIN

2. God commissioned Israel to display him to the world by
    being a holy (Hebrew, *kadosh* meaning "set apart for a mis-
    sion") nation distinct from the nations around them in dress,
    diet, morality, devotion to him, and compassion and concern
    for needy people. The Pharisees took God's command to be
    set apart to the extreme, but how might the following por-
    tions of Scripture have fueled their passion to be holy? (See
    Exodus 19:5 – 6; Leviticus 19:2; 20:7 – 8, 25 – 26; Deuteron-
    omy 14:2; 26:18 – 19; 28:9.)

3. What impact might Numbers 19:22; Psalm 1:1 – 3; 5:4 – 5; Isa-
    iah 52:11; and Ezekiel 22:23 – 26 have had on Pharisees who
    criticized Jesus for eating with "sinners"?

DID YOU KNOW?

What the Pharisees Believed

The Pharisees desired to raise the spiritual character of the Jewish people
and help them draw nearer to God. Most tried to be totally devoted to God.
They had many beliefs in common with Jesus. They believed in the physical
resurrection of the dead and a coming day of judgment followed by reward
or punishment. They anticipated the Messiah at any moment and believed in
angels. They believed God was all-wise, all-knowing, just, and merciful. They
taught that he loved his people and had called them to a life of obedience.
Pharisees also believed that everyone has the power to choose good or evil,
and that the Torah must be our guide in making that choice. The "yoke of

Torah" (or method of obeying) taught by the Pharisees, however, was a heavy burden that sometimes obscured the Torah they sought to obey.

Although they set high moral standards, not all Pharisees were godly and righteous. Some were so zealous for their oral interpretations that they violated the very letter of the Torah. Others focused so intently on obedience that they did not notice or care about needy people—a problem many of Jesus' followers also struggle with today. The truly faithful harshly condemned overemphasis on tiny details of obedience, particularly to human tradition, at the expense of the care and concern for others that the Torah demanded.

It's unfair and incorrect to paint all Pharisees with the brush of legalism and hypocrisy. Many were a powerful force for good among God's people. In many (perhaps most) respects, the theology of early Christians was similar to that of the Pharisees, and both groups worshiped in synagogues.

Reflection

Jesus came to carry out Israel's mission of being God's witness to an unclean world. He was truly holy, without any sin, and his holiness wasn't threatened by becoming involved in the lives of unclean people. In fact, he came to seek out lost sinners so that they could become clean.

In their passionate pursuit of holiness, some Pharisees became unwilling to engage the very people for whom they had been commissioned as priests. They failed to be and to display God's presence amidst those who needed to know him. Yet let's not be too critical. The Pharisees overemphasized separation at the expense of engaging their broken world, but most were faithful to obey the Text. If we shared some of the Pharisee's devotion to obedience, we would likely be much better witnesses of God in our world.

It isn't easy to strike the right balance between being set apart to obey God's commands and engaging in the world so that we reach those who are lost. As you read the following verses that show how this balance played out in the lives of God's people in the New Testament, consider how you might find a better balance in your life.

How important did the early Christians believe it was to avoid anything "unclean"? (See 2 Corinthians 6:17.)

What did God do to help one of his followers understand his role in reaching out to those who are unclean and in need of redemption? (See Acts 10:14, 27 – 28.)

What do the following situations reveal about the heart of Jesus to seek out the lost, needy, and unclean in order to display God's love for them? (See Matthew 14:13 – 14; 15:32; Mark 1:38 – 42.)

What commitment are you willing to make to obey God in everything so that you accurately display God to spiritually lost people around you?

What risks are you willing to take to seek out those who desperately need to be redeemed?

Memorize

But God demonstrates his own love for us in this: While we were still sinners, Christ died for us.

Romans 5:8

PROFILE OF A PEOPLE

Who Were the Sadducees?

Like the Pharisees, the Sadducees had roots in the time of the Hasmonaean dynasty. After the Israelites returned from Babylonian captivity, tradition held that the high priest must be of the tribe of Levi, family of Aaron, and family of Zadok — Solomon's high priest (1 Kings 2:35; Ezekiel 40:46). Descendants of this family (called *Zedukim*, "Sadducee" in English) and their supporters, many of whom were priests, became the temple authorities.

The Sadducees' authority was based on position and birth, rather than on the piety and knowledge of the Pharisees. Sadducees hated Pharisees because they believed that the synagogue and study of the Torah and its interpretations as a form of worship undermined the temple ritual. With Roman support, they could deal brutally with anyone who undermined the temple, its economy (their income), and its ritual. In their eyes, worship was an act of homage to the divine ruler, not an exercise in understanding.

The Sadducees were wealthy and politically active. Many were Hellenistic in lifestyle, although they faithfully maintained the temple rituals. Their power was largely based in Jerusalem and Judea through their majority in the Sanhedrin, the ruling religious council used by the Romans and Herods to govern the Jewish people. This gave them far greater influence than their small numbers (perhaps fewer than a thousand) justified.

The Sadducees contended that only the written Torah was authoritative. They rejected oral law completely and believed the prophets and other writings were of less value than the Torah. They denied a bodily resurrection and most Pharisaic doctrine regarding angels and spirits. They opposed the Pharisees in every way possible until the temple's destruction in AD 70, when the Sadducees ceased to exist.

Day Three | The Good Shepherd Seeks the Lost

The Very Words of God

> *Now the tax collectors and sinners were all gathering around to hear*
> *Jesus. But the Pharisees and the teachers of the law muttered, "This*
> *man welcomes sinners and eats with them." Then Jesus told them this*
> *parable: "Suppose one of you has a hundred sheep and loses one of*
> *them. Doesn't he leave the ninety-nine in the open country and go after*
> *the lost sheep until he finds it?"*

Luke 15:1–4

It may seem odd to us that Jesus responded to the Pharisees' mur-
muring about his interaction with sinners by telling a parable
that begins with a lost sheep. But there's no doubt that his story
of a shepherd and his lost sheep got everyone's attention. He was
speaking to people who were very familiar with shepherds and
their sheep. They knew that a lost sheep must be found or it will lie
under a bush or stand on a hillside and bleat until it dies of thirst or
is eaten by a predator. They must have wondered what kind of shepherd would lose a sheep in the hot, desolate wilderness.

Jesus was speaking to people who grew up knowing the Hebrew
Bible. They understood the metaphor of God being the Good Shepherd and Israel being his flock.[9] For generations God had expended
his never-ending love, protection, and provision on his people, caring for them as a shepherd cares for the flock. As a people, they had
experienced being lost sheep — sometimes because they had chosen
the wrong path, sometimes because their human shepherds had
been unfaithful. More than once they had been the lost sheep that
God found and restored to his loving care.

Jesus was also speaking to people who were intellectually and
spiritually curious. They studied the Torah faithfully, continually
questioning and debating among themselves in order to gain spiritual understanding and determine obedient behavior. Jesus' story of
the lost sheep and the seeking shepherd gave them much to think
about.

Bible Discovery

Jesus Shepherds His Flock

1. God defines the relationship between himself and his people through the image of a shepherd and his flock: Israel is God's flock, he is their shepherd.

   a. As you read through the following verses, what portrayal of God the Good Shepherd do you begin to see, and how does it affect your understanding of him? (See Psalm 28:8 - 9; 80:1 - 3; 100:3; Ezekiel 34:30 - 31.)

   b. What shepherd qualities does God display toward his people, and what do these qualities add to your experience of him? (See Psalm 23:1 - 6; 78:52 - 53; Isaiah 40:11; Ezekiel 34:16; Micah 7:14; and Zechariah 9:16.)

2. The Text portrays God as the Good Shepherd and recognizes leaders who represent God as his "undershepherds," as in Psalm 77:20: "You led your people like a flock by the hand of Moses and Aaron." God's human shepherds are entrusted to lead and care for his flock.

   a. Moses was the first person designated to be Israel's shepherd on the Lord's behalf. When he realized that he would no longer be with God's people to lead them, what did Moses entreat God to do? (See Numbers 27:15 - 23.)

    b.   What does this reveal about Moses' understanding of his role as God's undershepherd?

    c.   How important is the role of undershepherd for the well-being of God's people? (See 2 Samuel 24:17; 1 Chronicles 11:1 – 2; 21:17; Psalm 78:70 – 72; Jeremiah 3:14 – 15; 23:1 – 4.)

    d.   By the time of Jesus, Jewish people believed that all appointed and anointed leaders (kings and priests) were God's shepherds — including the high priest in the temple and local religious leaders such as rabbis and Pharisees. What are the risks to God's people, especially to lost sheep, when the undershepherds ignore or underestimate the serious nature of their responsibility?

3.   God holds his human shepherds responsible for his flock.[10] But all too often in Israel's history the shepherds who were supposed to act on God's behalf did not care for God's flock well. Read Jeremiah 23:1 – 8; 50:6 – 7; and all of Ezekiel 34.

    a.   In the chart provided, write down the offenses of the Ezekiel 34 shepherds.

The Text	Offenses Committed by God's Undershepherds
Ezek. 34:1 – 3	

Ezek. 34:4	
Ezek. 34:5–6	
Ezek. 34:8	
Ezek. 34:17–19	

b. What did God say about his unfaithful shepherds —
religious leaders who didn't care for his beloved sheep
according to his desire, who didn't lead them on paths of
righteousness? How would God, as Israel's Good Shepherd who never fails his sheep, respond? (See Jeremiah
23:1–8, 34–40.)

DID YOU KNOW?

Jesus Is the Good Shepherd

Jesus claimed to be the "good shepherd" (John 10:11, 14), a title that
belonged to God alone. Certainly Jesus demonstrated throughout his life
that he was the shepherd who would care for the sheep as God does, particularly in his willingness to die on the cross as an atoning sacrifice for his
sheep. Jesus pointed to the fact that he is not just a righteous shepherd, he
is the incarnate Good Shepherd — God in human form. In the minds of Jesus'
audience, such a shepherd would be the Messiah!

To acknowledge Jesus as the Good Shepherd is also to recognize that he
is Lord and King with absolute authority over his flock. It seems easier to
picture Jesus as our compassionate, caring Savior than as our eternal King
who expects us to obey him in everything we do. But to claim Jesus as our

Shepherd is also to declare him as our King. This is not simply an intellectual commitment; it's a daily act of faith. So if Jesus' audience recognized him as the shepherd mentioned in the parable of the lost sheep, they were reminded of his compassion for the flock and the expectation that they must obey him as their King.

4. Read Isaiah 53:6 and Ezekiel 34:1 – 10 and imagine that you are a Pharisee hearing Jesus tell this parable. You recognize that you are one of God's undershepherds, responsible for caring for his beloved flock. You know that if Jesus responded to your criticism with a parable about a shepherd and his sheep that he was saying something about you!

    a. How sobering would it be to realize that Jesus was eating with sinners because he recognized them as God's lost sheep and they needed a shepherd to find them?

    b. How might you have to reconsider your view of holiness in light of God's powerful criticism (Ezekiel 34) of shepherds who do not seek his lost sheep?

    c. Knowing the Scriptures very well (refresh your memory with Jeremiah 23:3 – 6), what might you be realizing about Jesus who is out welcoming sinners — seeking and gathering God's lost sheep?

DATA FILE

"He Refreshes My Soul"[11]

The portrayal of God as the Good Shepherd and his people as his flock is found throughout the Text and most powerfully described in Psalm 23. The phrase "he refreshes my soul" (Psalm 23:3) typically is understood to mean that God encourages us when we are discouraged. Although this is certainly a biblical teaching, the Hebrew word translated "refresh" comes from the root *shub* ("repent" or "cause to return"). So a more literal meaning would be the Lord refreshes—repents—our souls. *Shub* is also used in Jeremiah 23:3 to describe God taking action to become the shepherd, gather his lost sheep, and "bring them back" to the right path.

The image conveyed is of God gently directing his flock back onto the right path—"the paths of righteousness." Shepherds do this frequently. When a flock takes a wrong path, the shepherd moves closer, throwing pebbles alongside the sheep to direct them onto the right path. Although repentance is something the sinner—the lost sheep—must do in order to be forgiven by God, there is a sense in this psalm that God's leading is what causes a sinner to turn or repent.

Many times we repent due to some conviction that our lives have taken wrong paths. Yet if we look more closely, we discover that God—through a sermon, Bible study, verse we heard, the witness of someone else—led us to that conviction. Or perhaps consequences of sin or other circumstances brought us to the point of conviction of sin, confession, and return to God's path. We are found (saved) by grace alone and not by our own efforts.

God seeks lost sheep because they do not return on their own. They must be found. This is an important aspect of God's call to his people and Jesus' challenge to his audience. Lost sinners need God's involvement in their lives to bring them back to repentance. That's why those who claim to follow Jesus must become seekers of the lost, eating with sinners and welcoming them as he did. To isolate ourselves from ungodly people in order to be holy puts us in the place of the Pharisees in this story who resisted even the appearance of sin—which is what God desires—but in so doing refused to welcome sinners and "eat with them."

Reflection

Think of the effort that Jesus — the Good Shepherd — expended for us when we were lost sheep who could not find our way to God. Whereas the shepherd in Jesus' parable likely climbed rugged mountains in the desert to find a lost sheep, our Messiah had a much greater task. He emptied himself to take the form of a human and become the "Good Shepherd" — an act of grace beyond measure. He suffered things humans suffer — hunger and thirst, probably the loss of his father, mockery, rejection by the religious establishment, a friend's betrayal, the pain of flogging, and a brutal death on the cross. Possessing unbelievable grace, he bore the penalty for the sins of all lost sheep — the very pain of hell for the sake of his flock. Praise God!

Jesus did not wait for his sheep to return, or we would still be lost. He came to seek and save lost sheep. I pray that you are one who has been found. He also came to commission his followers to shepherd his flock. That's why Jesus challenged the Pharisees to join him in searching for his lost sheep. It doesn't matter where the sheep is or whether it is lost because it chose the wrong path or because a shepherd has been unfaithful; God wants his followers to be good shepherds who — no matter what the cost — follow Jesus' example and find his lost sheep.

> God still entrusts his flock to human shepherds. Read John 10:1 – 16, which describes the relationship between the Good Shepherd and his sheep. Take note of the qualities of Jesus the Good Shepherd and consider how his example might instruct and guide us as we seek to be faithful shepherds who go out and find lost sinners so that they might be restored to the Father's house.

The shepherd expended significant effort to find the sheep and carry it home. Then he had a party to celebrate. In our world today, what extraordinary effort are we willing to expend to "find" lost sinners who otherwise will not join God's family on their own?

Where should we go to find them?

How might we welcome lost sheep into our lives so that they will come to know their Good Shepherd?

How can we do a better job of celebrating sinners who are found *and* those who found them?

Memorize

He tends his flock like a shepherd: He gathers the lambs in his arms and carries them close to his heart; he gently leads those that have young.

Isaiah 40:11

Day Four | Rejoice! What Is Lost Has Been Found!

The Very Words of God

> *Or suppose a woman has ten silver coins and loses one. Does she not
> light a lamp, sweep the house and search carefully until she finds it?
> And when she finds it, she calls her friends and neighbors together and
> says, "Rejoice with me; I have found my lost coin." In the same way, I
> tell you, there is rejoicing in the presence of the angels of God over one
> sinner who repents.*

Luke 15:8 – 10

Bible Discovery

A Woman Finds Her Lost Coin

Jesus continued his parable with another "lost and found" story. This
time he chose a new character quite different from the desert shepherd — a woman who lost a small, but valuable, coin at home. In so
doing, he engaged more listeners. A person who didn't tend a flock
could relate to this woman while Jesus continued to emphasize his
original point to scholars who disapproved of his association with
"sinners."

The three-part parable we are studying shows how Jesus communicated well with all people.[12] People called him "rabbi" ("honored
teacher"); like other Jewish teachers Jesus told parables, made allu-
sions to Scripture by lifting a word or phrase from a Hebrew Bible
passage, traveled through their communities teaching, and men-
tored disciples in the "yoke of the kingdom of heaven." But Jesus
was unique in the way he drew all people into his teaching. Jesus
came to seek and to save those who are lost — everyone.

1. Jesus chose twelve young men to be disciples, but he did not
    limit his teaching to them. Notice how important it was that
    no one be excluded from his invitation to enter the kingdom
    of heaven and join him in seeking others who are lost.

a. According to Luke 10:39, who else "sat at the Lord's feet" — a phrase used to describe someone who studied with a rabbi?[13]

b. Who traveled with Jesus regularly — an unusual occurrence at that time? (See Luke 8:1 – 3.)

c. When people brought little children to Jesus so that he would bless them, how did his disciples respond, and why did Jesus rebuke them? (See Matthew 19:13 – 15; Mark 10:13 – 16; Luke 18:15 – 17.)

POINT TO PONDER

God's Mission to Seek and Redeem Is for Everyone

In a fascinating double parable, Jesus described his disciples' mission as being like a town on a hill or a lamp on a stand (Matthew 5:14 – 16). Scholars have noted that in the very traditional villages of Galilee, men built cities and women lit lamps. So it seems that Jesus passed on the mission of being his witness to a broken world to both men and women (and children as well).

2. The shepherd in the previous portion of Jesus' parable
    extended great effort to search for and bring home the one
    lost sheep of his flock of one hundred. The woman knew the
    lost coin was in her home. Even so, how much effort did she
    exert to find the one coin of the ten she owned? (See Luke
    15:8.)

    a. What do you think Jesus was suggesting about the value
        of lost sinners, whether they are to be found far away or
        close to home?[14]

    b. Considering that Jesus was speaking in part to Pharisees
        who were not joining him in searching for lost sinners,
        what do you think his phrase "doesn't she" adds to his
        message? (See Luke 15:8 and also 15:4.)

    c. As you consider these parallel parables, what else did
        Jesus say to help draw people into his story and fuel their
        desire to join him in searching for that which is lost? In
        what subtle ways did he point out that they were missing
        an opportunity to fulfill the very mission they sought to
        fulfill? (See Luke 15:3 – 10.)

DID YOU KNOW?
Searching for a Lost Coin

Galilean homes were made of dark stone with very few windows. In some rooms, floors were simply beaten earth or mud plaster. In others, larger cobblestones were laid that allowed any water that came in to drain away between the stones. People who heard Jesus' parable about the woman finding a small coin in her house understood that most rooms had little light and that a rough floor provided many hiding places for a lost coin. The only assistance a woman would have in her search would be a coarse broom made of straw or date palm stems and a small oil lamp that provided light from a single flame. Finding a lost coin would have been dusty, tiresome work.

A WOMAN SWEEPS A STONE FLOOR USING A TRADITIONAL BROOM.

3. After acknowledging to her community that she found the coin, what did the woman (like the shepherd) ask her community to do? (See Luke 15:9 – 10, and also 15:6 – 7.)

   a. What effort did the woman expend to find the coin?

   b. What do the seekers want to celebrate? (Hint: It's not just about the sheep or the coin that was found!)

   c. In what way would such a celebration put God on display?

Reflection

In the tight-knit social communities of the ancient Middle East, one person's loss was everyone's loss and everyone celebrated one person's good news. It must be the same in the community of redeemed people, the Father's house today. We each must value the lost, whoever and wherever they may be — not only when the lost person is our child, neighbor, brother, sister, or friend. Each one matters!

And we must learn to rejoice and celebrate when one is found. Jesus told us of the immense joy in heaven when the lost are found. All of heaven celebrates! It is a joy that must be shared — not just with an email, but with a party! And the celebration is not just for the one who is found, but for God who sacrificed even his Son — and for his faithful partners who seek the lost on his behalf.

The mission God has given to his partners in redemption is one of priceless joy. When the Pharisees decided it was more important to be holy and avoid sinners than it was to put God on display by welcoming them, they missed out on great joy.

To what extent do we miss out on that joy as well by standing on the sidelines and judging and criticizing instead of engaging in the lives of spiritually lost people?

What changes in perspective and action must we make in order to restore the joy of our Lord to the mission he has given us?

How might we, in our faith communities, do a better job of celebrating lost sinners who are brought into the Father's house? Of celebrating our gracious, forgiving God and his partners who faithfully seek his lost children?

Day Five | A Father Loses His Son

The Very Words of God

> *Jesus continued: "There was a man who had two sons. The younger one said to his father, 'Father, give me my share of the estate.' So he divided his property between them. Not long after that, the younger son got together all he had, set off for a distant country and there squandered his wealth in wild living."*
>
> *Luke 15:11 – 13*

Bible Discovery

The Greatest Loss of All

As we examine the beginning of the third portion of this parable — the climax, when a father "loses" his son — it is important to remember that all three stories are part of Jesus' response to the Pharisees' criticism, which is why we have considered them as one parable with three parts.[15] Luke reminded us of this by introducing the third story with "Jesus continued." So the themes and points Jesus emphasized in the first two stories should be affirmed and even expanded by the third. (We'll consider the last part of the third story in a later session.)

This parable hits close to home. The previous two were about possessions — a sheep and a coin. This one is about a lost son. It is about rejection of "the father's house," or *beth ab* and all it represents and the heartbreaking loss of relationship between a father and son.

Jesus' audience would likely have been shocked by the situation Jesus described.

1. In the first session of this series, we explored the patriarchal lifestyle of people in the Bible who lived as extended families in *beth ab*. Everything belonged to the family in perpetuity, and from one generation to the next the "patriarch" (father, or oldest male) used family resources to care for the family. As the firstborn son matured, he was trained to always seek the best interests of the *beth ab* in which he would one day become the patriarch. When the father died, the son would receive a majority of the family's estate, described in Deuteronomy 21:17 as a double share or portion, so that he would be able to care for the family. This was God's way of creating a community that cared for people in chaos and ensured there would never be a class of permanently poor people. This was still the practice for first century Jewish families. But in the third part of Jesus' parable, he described a *beth ab* in crisis. (See Luke 15:11 – 12.)

   a. What did the younger son demand of his father?

   b. What did his demand reveal about his relationship with his father, his view of family, his relationship with God, and God's plan to provide for extended family members?

2. Jesus' listeners would have expected the father to punish his younger son for dishonoring his family because that was what the law required (Deuteronomy 21:18 – 21).[16] But Jesus' story took an unexpected turn.

a. The father had a choice — whether or not to give his rebellious son the freedom to choose his own path, even if it meant rejecting his own father. What do you think motivated the father to make the choice he did?

b. To what extent does our heavenly Father give each of us freedom to choose our paths, even if we turn our backs to him?

3. After the son left, what indicates his complete rejection of everything his father and his house represented? (See Luke 15:13 – 16.)

Explain what you think Jesus' audience thought at this point in the story about the younger son and the lost sinners within their midst.

The previous parables concluded with the lost sheep and coin being found and celebrated. What do you think the chances are that Jesus' audience thought this parable would end in a similar way?

FOR GREATER UNDERSTANDING
The Family Crisis

The younger son's demand for his share of the estate would have shocked Jesus' audience.[17] Inheritances were for the benefit of the entire family, not "divided" as they normally are in our culture. Furthermore, the Torah instructed that the land (*nahala*) God entrusted to Jewish families in the days of Joshua must remain in the family. If it were lost to another member of the Jewish community, God gave specific instructions on how it eventually could be redeemed and returned to its rightful owner. Family property lost to Gentiles who were not bound by the Torah, however, was not likely to be returned. In first century Jewish communities, losing *nahala* to a Gentile was nearly unforgiveable and would result in the person who lost it being rejected by the whole community, including the family.

By asking for his "share" of the family "estate," the son was clearly rejecting the family heritage, tradition, and faith. When the son liquidated his "share" and took the proceeds away from the family, it was as if his father were dead. The son's actions would have shattered relationships in the family and broken his father's heart.

In a culture where one's honor is the most prized possession, the son humiliated his father in front of his family and the entire village, which was shamed before the entire region! The shame and dishonor to the village is beyond our Western imagination. I have asked Middle Eastern "patriarchs" what the effects of such a request would be today. They have always answered, "This would never happen." If it did, the pain would be worse than if the son had died. The family would be humiliated for generations; the son would be permanently expelled from the family—and, as one elderly father told me, likely from the village as well.[18]

We should note that the older son, the patriarch-in-training, did nothing to reconcile the situation.[19] Instead, he was content to take his own portion, seeming not to care about his brother's defiance, his father's shame, or the family's well-being. To add insult to injury, the younger son departed for a "distant country," which meant he went to the land of the Gentiles. Physically and spiritually, he could not be any farther away from the father's house.

Reflection

We will finish our study of the parable of the lost son in another session. Jesus' parable to this point has certainly given us — as it did for his audience — enough to think about. As a father, I find myself thinking about the younger son and his father. Surely the father loved his son deeply and showed great compassion and patience for him. Picture, if you will, the father looking after his son as he walked away from the *beth ab.*

His son had rejected his father and his family heritage. How had he rejected his God, too?

Do you imagine the son was still wearing his tassels? Or do you imagine that he took them off, not wanting to be identified with a value system he no longer held, or to be reminded of the God he was to obey and display to the world?

What do you think the father might have thought as he looked down at his own tassels and headed back to his *beth ab?*

The image of the father tugs at my heart. How is it possible for those of us who claim to follow Jesus to stand back and hold onto our holiness, comfort, and pride rather than seeking out and extending our Father's love toward his lost children who are living as if God were dead?

THE LOST SON: IN A FAR COUNTRY

After his death and resurrection Jesus told his disciples, "Go and make disciples of all nations" (Matthew 28:19). This "Great Commission," as it is called, is a continuation of the mission God gave the Israelites on Mount Sinai when he chose them to be his kingdom of priests, his holy nation. God called his people to be holy, to obey him so that they would mediate his presence and display him to all people. They were to be a light to Gentiles and make his name — his character, his reputation — known to all nations.[1]

So why, when Jesus sent out his disciples to share his message previously (Matthew 10:5 – 6), did he specifically instruct them to "not go among the Gentiles"? Apparently the mission to Gentiles would come after he finished training the twelve to "live as Jesus did."[2] In fact, Jesus focused his teaching on the Jewish people, drawing his message from God's ancient revelation in the Text. With notable exceptions, he gave most of his powerful lessons to those he called the "lost sheep of Israel" (Matthew 15:24).

In the process of reaching those lost sheep, Jesus spent time with "sinners" and "tax collectors," which greatly displeased some Pharisees who viewed "sinners" as unclean. It is easy to understand their reaction because they were fully committed to being holy (set apart) as God had commanded. In response to their concerns, Jesus told a parable containing three stories. The last one focused on a young Jewish son[3] who left home and went to a "far country" (KJV) — to the Gentiles.

Rather than going there as a priest to make his God known, this young man became involved with pagan Gentiles as part of his rejection of the faith of his family and community. So the pagans in the far country had a far greater influence on shaping him than he had on them. Jesus provided few details concerning the "far country." He simply said that the young man lived a "reckless" life (ESV), lost all his money, and became homeless and hungry. Eventually it seemed to him that returning home was a better option than starving.

For ancient Jewish sages, including Jesus, telling parables was a common form of instruction,[4] so Jesus' hearers were practiced in understanding their meanings. For us, understanding a parable is more challenging because points often remain unexplained. Without a specific answer in the Text, we must seek to discern a parable's meaning by good scholarship and by our interpretation. Sometimes the Text reveals listeners' reactions, which helps us to understand Jesus' point.[5] One helpful "tool" is to ask: "What did the original audience — the hearers — understand when Jesus told this particular parable?"

When applying this question to the "prodigal" story, I asked: *What did Jesus' audience understand a far country to be? What did they think the young man faced — and what did a "reckless" life involve? What did hearers believe caused him to want to return home, and what would he face when he returned?* Although the Text doesn't answer these questions directly, it is my opinion that Jewish history reveals what Jewish people thought about pagans.

Based on insights into the Gentile mind and lifestyle, let's consider what the prodigal likely experienced as he entered the pagan world, which was so different from his Jewish community. Our exploration will give us opportunities to consider our walk with God as well. All Jesus followers have been commissioned — as God's people always have been — to be light in a "far country." Our mission is no different from that of Joseph, Jonah, or Daniel who lived in such a world — or Paul, who traveled from one "far country" to another. Sustained by the Holy Spirit and the community of Jesus followers, we are to live among the "pagans" in order to seek out the lost. So let us consider the temptations we face to live "reckless" lives and how to better understand and seek out people who choose this path.

Opening Thoughts (3 minutes)

The Very Words of God

> *So do not worry, saying, "What shall we eat?" or "What shall we drink?" or "What shall we wear?" For the pagans run after all these things, and your heavenly Father knows that you need them. But seek first his kingdom and his righteousness, and all these things will be given to you as well.*
>
> **Matthew 6:31 – 33**

Think About It

We live in a culture that religious Jews of Jesus' day surely would call a "far country." Many, if not most, people reject obedience to God's commandments that display his character, his love, and bring blessing to other people. Instead, they live by a different set of values and follow whichever rules yield the greatest pleasure, power, or possessions for themselves.

What are some of the temptations that we, as Jesus' followers today, are drawn to in our "far country"? How obvious or subtle are these temptations? Which do you think have the most serious consequences when we give in to them?

DVD Notes (29 minutes)

The message of the gate

Will he choose the tassels or the "far country"?

Exciting amusements

Magnificent temples

Enticing worship of gods

Material possessions

Destitute and thinking of home

How will the lost son be found?

DVD Discussion (9 minutes)

1. This study was filmed at Jerash (first-century, Gerasa) in Jordan between the capital city of Amman and the Syrian border. The wadi Jabbok (a seasonal river bed) runs through the city, now as well as in the first century. This wadi is where Jacob met his brother, Esau, centuries before Jesus' time.

    Locate the following sites on the map below: Jerusalem, Sea of Galilee, Nazareth, Qatzrin, Bethsaida, Decapolis, Jerash, Philadelphia (Amman), Scythopolis (Beth Shan).

    Although Jesus didn't provide a specific location for his Luke 15 parable, the cities of the Decapolis certainly offered the lifestyle and temptations to which the young man was drawn. Imagine how Jews who were obedient to God's commands would stand out as a light in that world!

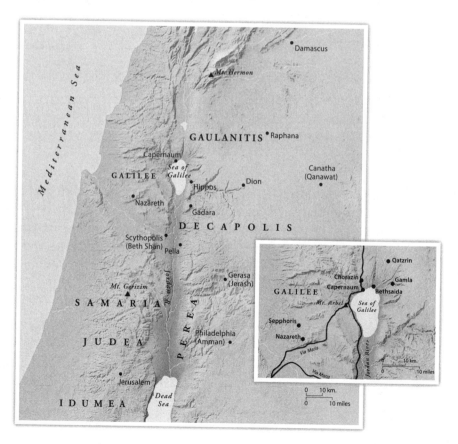

2. When you imagined the Prodigal Son in a "far country," what kind of a place did you think it would be?

What about Jerash, as representative of cities in the Decapolis, was most informative or impressive to you?

What do you think it would have been like for a young Jewish man to go from a village similar to Qatzrin to a city like Jerash?

What would your concern be if one of your children were to make a similar journey?

3. We tend to think that our culture is more evil and enticing than those that have come before it. Now that you have a picture of the power, cultural sophistication, enticing amusements, wealth, and immoral debauchery associated with religious worship that were part of daily life in Jerash and other cities of the Decapolis, has your perspective changed? If so, how?

4. It was easy to be taken in by the excitement, beauty, abundance of material goods, and status that the lifestyle of Jerash offered without realizing that there was a worldview of another kingdom behind it. Yet, if the lost son was still wearing his tassels in the "far country," he had an ever-present reminder of God's kingdom.

    a. How much attention do you think the lost son paid to his tassels, and how might he have struggled in choosing whether to follow the calling of the tassels or the calling of the "far country"?

    b. What impact do you think wearing tassels would have on a person who wanted to obey God's every command and lived in a place similar to Jerash?

    c. How aware are we of the presence of the other kingdom in our modern culture? What do we encounter in everyday life that has the power to pull us in without our even realizing it?

Small Group Bible Discovery and Discussion (14 minutes)

A Lost Son in a "Far Country"

Jesus' brilliant three-story parable reaches its climax when a father "loses" his younger son.[6] Having rejected his family's values and beliefs, and dishonored his father, the "lost" son set out for a distant country — a "far country." In parables of the Jewish tradition, such a destination is generally associated with the land of the Gentiles simply because the Promised Land God gave Israel was small — about the size of New Jersey. So any land far away would be Gentile, the land where pagans lived.

Jesus obviously intended to highlight a pagan location because the rebellious son was soon feeding pigs, a clear indication that he was in the land of the pagans. Regardless of how many miles away this land was, in Jesus' mind there was great distance between its pagan lifestyle and that of the Pharisees to whom Jesus told this parable. The Greek text implies that the son "traveled away from his people." That was true — physically and spiritually.[7]

1. God raised up Israel to be a holy witness to the "far countries" of their world — to people estranged from the "Father's house." In what ways were the younger son's reasons for going there dramatically different from God's commission at Mount Sinai for his people to be his holy "priests" to all nations? (See Exodus 19:3 – 6; Isaiah 42:6.)

PROFILE OF A CULTURE
The Decapolis: Hellenism in a "Far Country"

Greek settler-soldiers of the Ptolemaic and Seleucid kingdoms founded many of the cities that became known as the Decapolis (Greek: *deca*, ten; *polis*, city). These kingdoms were sections of Alexander the Great's empire divided among his generals after his death. His dream of "hellenizing" (making Greek) the entire world to be under the influence of Greek culture in religion, language, philosophy, political structure, and values did not die with him. Ensuing dynasties were as devoted to Greek ideals as he had been, each integrating local customs and practices into their particular cultures.

The Maccabean revolt, and the support of this revolt by Hasidim fighters fiercely devoted to Yahweh and the Torah, was in large part a reaction to attempts by Greek-thinking kingdoms to convert Jews to their pagan values and practices. Their victory was short-lived, however. In 64–63 BC, the Roman general Pompey brought the entire Near East under Rome's dominion. He incorporated the Greek cities east of the Sea of Galilee and one city (Beth Shan—renamed Scythopolis—that was west of the Jordan River, just south of the sea) into the league of cities known as the Decapolis. Resentful of the attempts by religious Jews to convert them during the

THE MANY FOUNTAINS OF THE NYMPHAEUM IN JERASH PROVIDED WATER FOR THE PEOPLE.

AN UNUSUAL OVAL FORUM IN JERASH DISPLAYS THE GREATNESS OF THE GRECO-ROMAN CULTURE.

Maccabean period (167–63 BC), many pagan residents were pleased to have Rome's help in resisting the seemingly outdated worldview of the Jews.

For much of its history, the Decapolis comprised more than ten cities, yet it still retained this designation. Many are familiar to New Testament readers: Damascus, Philadelphia (modern Amman), Scythopolis (Beth Shan), Gadara (Gadarenes), Pella, and Gerasa (Jerash). Hippos (Susita) overlooked the Sea of Galilee from the east. The Decapolis was on the Roman Empire's eastern frontier in what is modern-day Jordan, Syria, and Israel. These cities were centers of Greco-Roman culture and linked together because of their language, culture, location, and political status. As free city-states, they operated within Rome's administrative structure, had much local autonomy, and had jurisdiction over the surrounding countryside, including control of the trade route from Arabia to Damascus.

Desiring thoroughly Hellenistic Roman culture to prevail throughout its empire, the Roman government encouraged growth in the Decapolis. A network of paved Roman roads strengthened ties among the cities, and each city had a Roman-style grid of streets based on main streets called *cardo* and *decumanus*. To unify the people, they introduced the cult for the worship of the Roman emperor and built small temples (*kalybe*) dedicated to the emperor that were unique to the region.

The Romans also built many buildings for institutions that brought the values of Hellenism to daily life. Theaters produced dramas portraying the myths of Greek and Roman gods. These dramas contained erotic themes and were performed in connection with religious festivals that included sacrifices to various gods. In gymnasiums, the Greek educational institutions, students practiced the Greek ideal of training both body and mind. They studied the philosophy of classical Greece, received athletic training, and competed— naked—in athletic events. Stadiums hosted public athletic contests. Temples honored local gods. The architecture was stunning, and the marble streets, mosaic floors, running water, and fountains must have awed people from surrounding villages.

In the cities of the Decapolis and much of the known world, Hellenism influenced everyday life as people adopted Greek ways and established Greek cultural institutions. Greek even became the common tongue of the economic world. So, it's not surprising that faithful Jews struggled to maintain their God-focused beliefs in the midst of such tempting attractions.

At its core, Hellenism was humanism. It glorified human beings and portrayed the human body as the ultimate in physical beauty. Truth could be known only through the human mind, and pleasure was a crucial goal. Hellenism's values permeated the gymnasium and its system of education, theater, and arena games. The majestic Romanized forms of Hellenistic architecture in the cities of the Decapolis may have seemed harmless enough, but its temples glorified the excesses of pleasure.

It fell to the faithful Jews to resist these cultural institutions and pagan values. As a result, the Pharisees adopted increasingly detailed laws to remain faithful to Torah; the Zealots resisted Hellenism more violently; the Essenes withdrew into isolated communities; the Sadducees, while maintaining the prescribed temple rituals, often became as Hellenistic as the pagans. In the Decapolis, the worldviews of Hellenistic Greeks and Torah-following Jews clashed.

2. After Jesus ascended to heaven, his disciples went to the "far country" with the good news of redemption. Their writings were intended to instruct, encourage, and strengthen communities of Jesus followers who lived in the Gentile world and give us a picture of the lifestyle that the lost son chose when he renounced his heritage, faith, and family.

    a. As you read through these passages, note the practices and characteristics of the pagan lifestyle.

The Text	The Pagan Lifestyle of Gentiles
Acts 21:25	
Rom. 1:28–32;13:13	
Gal. 5:19–21	
Col. 3:5–10	
1 Peter 4:3–4	
Rev. 2:14	

    b. In Jewish thought, the three great sins of Gentiles, who did not acknowledge the Lord as their King, were idolatry, adultery, and bloodshed. What instructions related to these did Paul give to Jesus' early followers? (See Colossians 3:5 - 10.)

3. Read Numbers 15:38 - 41. At Mount Sinai, God commissioned Israel to be his kingdom of priests and later commanded them to wear tassels on the corners of their robes to remind

them to be set apart so that they would display his character to all nations.

a. What was the reason they were to wear their tassels, and what specific behaviors did God want them to avoid? (See Numbers 15:39.)

b. If the lost son was wearing his tassels, what do you think he felt as he entered the Gentile world and realized that the dominant motivation was the very thing God instructed his people to avoid?

c. How do you think Gentiles responded as they observed this Jewish young man embracing their lifestyle, and how might it have influenced their view of his God?

4. Throughout Israel's history God's people struggled to fulfill their mission while living in close proximity to the "far country." At times they became like the pagan nations; at other times they were so righteously insulated they had no witness to those God longed to bring back into his family. As Jesus followers today, we face the same struggle. In which ways do you see Christians:

a. Moving away from faithfulness to God and choosing (perhaps blindly) "Gentile" attitudes, values, and actions?

b. Isolating themselves from secular people and thus losing opportunities to display God's character to his lost children in our communities, schools, and workplaces?

Faith Lesson (4 minutes)

God chose Israel to be his people and commissioned them to be a kingdom of priests (Exodus 19:3 – 6) who would demonstrate his character by how they lived in the world. In that same commission, God commanded his people to be obedient and holy; worship him alone; and care for needy widows, orphans, and strangers. By doing so, they would fulfill God's promise that all nations would be blessed through the descendants of Abraham (Genesis 12:1 – 3).

It wouldn't be easy to avoid the influence of unclean pagan practices and ideas while at the same time interacting with pagans so that they would come to know Israel's God. God's people often grew complacent, corrupt, and fell prey to the temptations of their pagan neighbors. On the other hand, the Galileans who heard Jesus' three-part parable were likely quite insulated from the world. The question for us is, where on that spectrum do we fall, and how do we get to where God would have us be?

1. According to Jesus' words in Matthew 6:25 – 34, what differences exist between God's people who are faithful and obedient and Gentiles whose lives are dominated by the pursuit of power, pleasure, and leisure though the accumulation of wealth?

2. In what ways do we live as if "the good life" depends on our possessions, leisure activities, fame, beauty, etc. rather than being consumed by the desire to be an instrument of God's kingdom and passionately live obedient lives so that other people will be drawn to the true God?

3. In what way(s) does our pursuit of pleasure and material things influence our willingness to seek the lost, to sacrifice for the good of the needy, and to express God's compassion for those who suffer?

4. It's easy to point accusing fingers at the prodigal (as well as the Pharisees), but what if the Gentiles Jesus had in mind in his parable include twenty-first century Gentiles who live all around us? What would be Jesus' message to us about our priorities, our choices, and our lifestyle?

5. How might we, like God's ancient people who wore tassels, be reminded continually to obey him and by our holy lives display him to people around us who do not yet know (experience) him?

Closing (1 minute)

Read Deuteronomy 6:10 – 12 aloud together: "When the Lord your God brings you into the land he swore to your fathers, to Abraham, Isaac and Jacob, to give you — a land with large, flourishing cities you did not build, houses filled with all kinds of good things you did not provide, wells you did not dig, and vineyards and olive groves you did not plant — then when you eat and are satisfied, be careful that you do not forget the Lord, who brought you out of Egypt, out of the land of slavery."

Now pray, thanking God for the blessings he provides, including material things, and for his daily provision. Thank him for the community of believers who can encourage us to stand firm against the evil one's temptations. Ask him for a mind and heart that always remembers him and honors his ways. Pray that when we are satisfied we will be faithful to his commands, have compassion to seek the lost, and exercise wisdom to choose the right path.

Memorize

When the Lord your God brings you into the land he swore to your fathers, to Abraham, Isaac and Jacob, to give you — a land with large, flourishing cities you did not build, houses filled with all kinds of good things you did not provide, wells you did not dig, and vineyards and olive groves you did not plant — then when you eat and are satisfied, be careful that you do not forget the Lord, who brought you out of Egypt, out of the land of slavery.

Deuteronomy 6:10 – 12

Restoring the Lost to the Father's House

In-Depth Personal Study Sessions

Day One | A Light for the Gentiles

The Very Words of God

> *Then Paul and Barnabas answered them boldly: "We had to speak the word of God to you first. Since you reject it and do not consider yourselves worthy of eternal life, we now turn to the Gentiles. For this is what the Lord has commanded us: 'I have made you a light for the Gentiles, that you may bring salvation to the ends of the earth.'"*
>
> **Acts 13:46–47**

Bible Discovery

Jesus: Preparing Israel to Be a Light to the Gentiles

Christians often believe that Jesus came to bring salvation to the Gentiles. Certainly his life, redemptive death, and resurrection provide the only hope of salvation for Jews and Gentiles alike, yet Jesus primarily focused his life and teaching on the Jewish community. He was, after all, a Jew born to parents who could trace their heritage back to Abraham (Matthew 1).

Jesus lived, talked, acted, and worshiped like a Jew. His words, actions, and teaching methods as a rabbi were in keeping with the customs, traditions, and religion of the Semitic culture into which he was born. He became part of a race of people whom God had chosen to carry his name — his character, his reputation — to the entire world. As one of them, he came to restore that mission to God's chosen people. He carried out the mission on Israel's behalf, or as some have said, "He became Israel with them."

1. What did elderly Simon, a righteous and faithful Jew, prophesy when he saw the infant Jesus, and how would Jesus fulfill God's promise to Abraham? (See Luke 2:25 – 32; Genesis 12:1 – 3.)

2. Moses brought together the twelve tribes of Israel and led them to Mount Sinai where God commissioned them to be his partners in redeeming his world. What did God promise he would do for Israel, and how did Jesus show through his selection of disciples that he was the fulfillment of that promise? (See Deuteronomy 18:15 – 19; Matthew 4:18 – 22; 10:2 – 4.)

3. Jesus said on more than one occasion that his mission was to the lost sheep of Israel (Matthew 10:1 – 6; 15:21 – 28). So it should not surprise us that Jesus called God's people to faithfulness in the mission they had been given at Mount Sinai. This, in fact, is what the three-part parable we have been studying was about. What did Jesus say he was commissioned to be and that his disciples also were to be? (See Isaiah 42:6; Matthew 5:14; John 9:5.)

4. Whereas most of Jesus' ministry focused on teaching the Jewish community, the New Testament gospels of Matthew, Mark, and Luke reveal that Jesus ministered in the Decapolis

region on several occasions. Also, some Gentiles found out about Jesus and were drawn to him — some coming long distances to see him. As you read the following passages about Jesus' interaction with Gentiles, notice where Jesus was, who he interacted with, and what impact he had on their experience of God.

Matthew 4:23 - 25 (Note the places mentioned on the map earlier in session.)

Matthew 15:21 - 28; Mark 7:24 - 30

Mark 7:31 - 37

5. What do you think Jesus' disciples discovered about being a light to the Gentiles as they witnessed him making God's name known through these interactions? (See Exodus 20:7; 1 Chronicles 16:8.)

Reflection

As God's kingdom of priests, Israel was to be a light to the Gentiles and make his name known. This meant more than simply telling others what God's name was. It meant making God's character and reputation known to all people on the earth. They were to increase his reputation by the righteous way they lived.

Jesus came to carry out the same mission and to pass it on to his disciples. At Passover before he was betrayed, Jesus prayed, "Righteous Father, though the world does not know you, I know you, and they know that you have sent me. I have made you known to them, and will continue to make you known in order that the love you have for me may be in them and that I myself may be in them" (John 17:25 – 26). This is Jesus' declaration that he had lived and taught in such a way that his disciples had come to know the very character and nature of God. They were prepared to "hallow" God's name — to make his reputation known.

To hallow (Hebrew, *kiddush ha shem*) God's name means to increase the honor given God's name or reputation by the things we do or say. So when we pray the Lord's prayer (Matthew 6:9 – 13) and say "hallowed be your name, your kingdom come, your will be done," we are making a powerful statement of commitment to the mission of making God's character and reputation known to everyone.

When Moses' father-in-law heard the story of God delivering his people from Egypt, he praised the God of the Hebrews. That is *kiddush ha shem* — hallowing the name of God so that others know him and are drawn to him. This is the central mission God has given to his people. When we speak against injustice; work for the good of society; act with compassion for the poor, the homeless, the unborn, the alien, the lonely, the prisoner; when we work for peace; when we alleviate suffering — we hallow God's name. We don't need to be rich or powerful, simply obedient to God in helping to change our broken world.

What are you doing in your world to hallow God's name?

What can you help your faith community to do in order to hallow God's name?

The truth is that far too often God's people have profaned (Hebrew, *hillul hashem*) God's name. To profane God's name is to do anything that would lessen his reputation. Whenever we act disobediently, we defile God's name, his reputation is dishonored, and the light to the Gentiles is darkened. God takes his reputation so seriously that it is the only one of the Ten Commandments that carries a grave punishment — "the Lord will not hold anyone guiltless who misuses his name" (Exodus 20:7).

In what ways might you be defiling God's reputation — displaying a false image of God's nature — in your work, among your friends and neighbors, in your marriage and family relationships, in your responsibility to care for the marginalized, in your use of resources?

Memorize

But I have raised you up for this very purpose, that I might show you my power and that my name might be proclaimed in all the earth.

Exodus 9:16

Day Two | Kingdoms in Contrast

The Very Words of God

> *Jesus called them together and said, "You know that those who are*
> *regarded as rulers of the Gentiles lord it over them, and their high*
> *officials exercise authority over them. Not so with you. Instead,*
> *whoever wants to become great among you must be your servant, and*
> *whoever wants to be first must be slave of all. For even the Son of Man*
> *did not come to be served, but to serve, and to give his life as a ransom*
> *for many."*
>
> **Mark 10:42 – 45**

Bible Discovery

Jesus Teaches the Ways of the Kingdom of Heaven

Imagine growing up in a Galilean village that has no running water,
no magnificent temples to numerous gods, no stadium for athletic
events, and no ruling kings or nobles. Instead, the synagogue is the
primary hub of activity — for worship, religious study and debate,
and children's schooling. And the extended family provides the core
social structure of the community. Righteous living by loving God
and serving others according to his commands is everyone's primary
goal. That's the world the lost son in Jesus' parable knew ... and left.

What do you think it was like for that young man to walk into the
"far country" where the values and goals of Gentiles ruled? The culture of the pagans who dominated the Gentile world was from the
beginning based on the nature of the "evil one" who preached the
gospel of the "god named me."[8] This worldview promoted a lifestyle
that pursued power, pleasure, and leisure. The goal was to achieve
enough power (economic, political, social) to freely enjoy whatever
pleasures someone desired. It assigned value to people based on
power, accomplishment, accumulation, and beauty. The more of
these a person acquired, the more worth that person had.

It may surprise us, but Jesus did not criticize the brutality of Rome or speak against the immorality of the worship of Roman gods. Instead, he bluntly challenged his disciples to not be like those Gentiles! He knew that the objective for the Gentiles was to be served — from the slave who served everyone to the emperor whom everyone served. So he taught that such desires have no place in the kingdom of heaven, no place in the hearts of his disciples who were to live as he lived.

1. Despite their desire to follow Jesus, it was tempting for his disciples to get caught up in the mad pursuits of the world in which they lived. What did two of his disciples request that reflected the value placed on honor and authority in the Roman world? (See Matthew 20:20 - 25; Luke 22:24; Mark 10:35 - 40.)

   What contrast between the values of the kingdom of this world and the kingdom of heaven did Jesus point out in his reply? (See Matthew 20:25 - 28; Luke 22:25 - 27; Mark 10:42 - 45.)

   What did Jesus teach by word and example that refuted selfish demands and reinforced what the servant lifestyle of his kingdom is all about? (See Matthew 19:13 - 15; 23:11; Mark 1:35 - 39; 3:7 - 12; Luke 9:10 - 17; 14:12 - 13.)

   What did Paul and Peter later emphasize to their "disciples" that reveals they got it — they learned and took to heart the values of the kingdom of heaven? (See Galatians 5:13 - 15; 1 Peter 5:1 - 7.)

2. Even the prayers of the Romans were a pursuit to gain the upper hand. They would recite long lists of their gods' names again and again,[9] believing that doing so would ensure a favorable response. In contrast, what did Jesus teach was important to pray about, and how do such prayers reflect the priorities of his kingdom? (See Matthew 6:7 - 13.)

Reflection

The lifestyle of the kingdom of God is a calling to service. It does not demand for itself but gives to those in need. It does not hold tightly to blessings but uses them to bless others. The power of such a life — not political, economic, or military power — changes the world. Only by imitating Jesus and taking the form of a servant and expending ourselves for the benefit of others are we truly his disciples. That was Jesus' message to all who would seek to walk as he walked. It was a walk that the prophets foretold.

Read Isaiah 53. Carefully note the many ways Jesus, the King of Kings and the fulfillment of this prophecy, lived according to values that were unheard of in the kingdoms of this world.

Day Three | God Raised Up a Kingdom of Priests

The Very Words of God

> *May the God who gives endurance and encouragement give you the same attitude of mind toward each other that Christ Jesus had, so that with one mind and one voice you may glorify the God and Father of our Lord Jesus Christ. Accept one another, then, just as Christ accepted you, in order to bring praise to God.*
>
> *Romans 15:5–7*

Bible Discovery

God's Mission Is a Community Endeavor

When the lost son in Jesus' parable went to a "far country," he left behind his own people. Although he may not have valued it, he cut himself off from the loving support of his family and community relationships. In the minds of the Jews listening to Jesus' parable, it would be only a matter of time before he lost his way.

In the ancient Jewish world, as it still is in much of the Middle East today, family and community relationships were the central focus of life. People thought first of how their actions might affect the community and were willing to sacrifice their individual desires for the benefit of that community. This is what God intended. He did not want his people to live as individuals. From the beginning, he wanted them to live in caring, supportive communities where they could experience the joy found in the community of the Lord.

Let's consider what often happens when God's people lose the support of the community of faith, when they lose their "accountability group."

1. After Abraham assumed responsibility for his nephew, Lot, they lived as a large, extended family community. Eventually they became such a large group that conflict arose between their hired workers.

a. To keep peace in the family, what did Abraham propose and what choice did Lot make that affected him, his family, and later all of Israel? (See Genesis 13:5 – 12.)

b. When he separated from Abraham, what types of people did Lot "hang around with"? (See Genesis 13:13.)

c. What location — where key business, judicial, administrative, and other dealings occurred — shows that Lot had become an influential leader in his new city? (See Genesis 19:1 – 5.)

d. What indicates his attempt to live according to the priorities of God's kingdom, and what indicates that he struggled to do so? (See Genesis 19:3 – 10.)

e. After God delivered Lot and his two daughters from the destruction of Sodom and Gomorrah, what do we learn about how the pagan worldview of those cities had affected his daughters? (See Genesis 19:30 – 38; 1 Kings 11:33.)

2. What do these verses reveal about the blessings of God-centered community, and the desolation of losing it? (See Ruth 1:1 – 5, 16 – 17; Psalms 122; 133; Proverbs 15:22; 25:12.)

3. God's intent in bringing his people out of Egypt, training them in the desert, calling them at Mount Sinai, and providing his presence in the tabernacle was to raise up a kingdom (not just a prince or two) of priests, a holy nation (not just a neighborhood) to mediate his presence to a broken world.

    a. What did God command his people to do that encouraged the building and sustaining of a community of faith in Israel? (See Numbers 9:1 – 3; Deuteronomy 16:10 – 15.)

    b. What else did God command the Israelites to do that brought like-minded people together as a community, promoted accountability, and in part displayed God to people outside the "Father's house"? (See Numbers 15:38 – 40.)

4. God's desire for his people to be a kingdom of priests, a holy nation, a community of faithful servants did not end with Israel. Why is it important for followers of Jesus today to be a community — the body of Christ — not just "solo" saints trying to make it on their own? (See Luke 17:1 – 3; Acts 15:32; 1 Corinthians 12:14 – 20, 27; 1 Thessalonians 5:11; 1 Peter 2:4 – 5.)

5. What did the early believers realize about how they were to relate to one another in community? How would their community life increase God's character and reputation in the world? (See Acts 2:42 – 47; 1 Thessalonians 4:9 – 10; 1 Peter 2:17.)

Reflection

The Acts 2 account of the fellowship Jesus' followers shared is a powerful image of God's flawed but faithful partners living out their calling as a community — God's royal priesthood. Together they devoted themselves to teaching, fellowship, and prayer. They shared; they gave; they were filled with awe and joy at the wonder of God's kingdom coming to reign on earth. They made God's name known and people were drawn to him every day.

What would it mean to you to be part of such a community?

Imagine what it would have been like for the younger son who went to a "far country" to lose the support of his family and community relationships. How much impact do you think that isolation had on him — and his choices? Why?

When you are tired, stressed, angry, hungry, lonely ... what kinds of choices do you make on your own? Why?

In what ways might you reach out to like-minded Jesus followers to begin building a community where each one is embraced, encouraged, and supported in living out the mission to which Jesus calls us?

Memorize

As a prisoner for the Lord, then, I urge you to live a life worthy of the calling you have received. Be completely humble and gentle; be patient, bearing with one another in love. Make every effort to keep the unity of the Spirit through the bond of peace.

Ephesians 4:1 – 3

Day Four | Squandering His Wealth in Wild Living

The Very Words of God

Those who want to get rich fall into temptation and a trap and into many foolish and harmful desires that plunge people into ruin and destruction. For the love of money is a root of all kinds of evil. Some people, eager for money, have wandered from the faith and pierced themselves with many griefs.

1 Timothy 6:9 – 10

Bible Discovery

The Temptations of the "Far Country"

Jesus made it clear that his people are to be consumed by the desire to be an instrument of the kingdom of heaven, seeking by obedient living to extend God's reign so that others will be drawn to him. The Lord will provide for the daily concerns of people who live in such a way. However, this was not the consuming passion of the Gentile world — as the lost son would discover.

There were many temptations in the Gentile world that could consume him — spiritually, sexually, and financially. And he had the wealth — at least for a time — that allowed him to choose the lifestyle that most appealed to him. We don't know from Jesus' parable the details of what he chose, but we do know that he "squandered" his inheritance on "wild living" (NIV), "reckless living" (ESV), or "riotous living" (KJV). The Greek phrase used in Luke 15:13, *zon asotos*, implies uncontrolled, wasteful, profligate, extravagant, expensive, or squandering behavior. Traditionally it has meant that he became involved in various immoral actions, particularly sexual immorality. Certainly the "far country" offered that! Let's consider the possible meaning of "wild living" in the context of the Decapolis.

1. The entire Gentile world, and certainly the cities of the Decapolis, was known for the worship of many pagan gods including the "divine" emperor. Romans built temples for their gods everywhere. No matter which city the prodigal chose, he likely encountered a temple to Zeus, the king of all gods; a temple to Dionysus, the god of wine whose worshipers became notoriously intoxicated, ate raw meat, and committed sexual immorality of all kinds; a temple to the goddess Artemis, whose sexually immoral worship was renowned; and the list could go on and on.

    a. What commands and warnings did God give to his people concerning gods such as these? (See Exodus 20:3; Deuteronomy 12:29 – 32; Jeremiah 7:3 – 10.)

b.   What kinds of wickedness did the worship of these gods promote, and might these practices be considered "wild living" that would consume all of a person's resources? Why or why not?

DID YOU KNOW?

Because of their previous exile and suffering, idolatry had ceased being a temptation for most Jews by Jesus' time. Nevertheless, the reality of idolatry was a significant issue. Roman authorities often mocked and even persecuted people for their devotion to the Lord alone. To the Jewish people, idolatry was the root of evil because wherever the Lord's kingship was not recognized and another deity was honored in his place, every kind of immorality, perversity, and depravity reigned. In fact, the sages explained the evil and immorality that was the norm for the Gentile lifestyle was due to their rampant idolatry.

2.   The desire for material wealth can become our master, compelling us to pursue and store up treasure for ourselves. Read Matthew 6:19 – 34.

a.   What better alternative to the mad pursuit of wealth does Jesus offer?

b.   Which worries of life can lead us to store up treasure for ourselves, and what more important thing than "stuff" does it keep us from cultivating and sharing?

c. What are the differences Jesus points out between the pursuit of material gain and the pursuit of God's kingdom?

Pursuit of Material Gain	Pursuit of God's Kingdom

d. Which "kingdom" do you want to pursue as your master, and why?

FOR GREATER UNDERSTANDING

The Lost Son's Materialism

In the Greek Text, the word *asotosthe* used to describe the lifestyle of the lost son can be translated "wasteful" or "squandered" and literally means "scattered."[10] This conveys the implication of extravagant, expensive, or luxurious living. Kenneth Bailey, in his exceptional study of this parable, notes that Eastern versions emphasize the younger son's wasteful, spendthrift lifestyle, not sexual immorality. Luke 15:14 reads, "After he had spent everything ..." Bailey wrote that the word translated "spent everything" means "waste," "squander," or "spend freely."[11] In other words, he overspent on things he could not afford. In modern terms, he went over his credit limit.

This understanding certainly doesn't limit the meaning of the prodigal's rejection of his faith to overspending. Perhaps Jesus chose to use terms broad enough to include any rejection of one's faith that any prodigal might choose. Yet not to include the idea that the younger son was drawn to material wealth and sought happiness in what he could "consume" and "own" is to overlook a sinful lifestyle that is prevalent—and a major failure—in the community of faith today. We too seek contentment and security in possessions and consumption. We too pursue material wealth—things that soon own us and cause us to lose sight of the purpose for which God redeemed us.

3.　In another parable, Jesus spoke of a farmer (certainly a metaphor for God) sowing seed (the Word of God) that fell on various kinds of soil. Depending on where the seed fell, it either failed to grow or became fruitful. Read the parable in Mark 4:1 – 20, taking particular note of verses 18 – 19.

　　a.　What choked the sprouting seed so it produced no fruit?

　　b.　Jesus warned that pursuing wealth and possessions is deceitful and easily becomes so overpowering that his disciples would have no fruit in their lives. This story is in a sense a critique of the prodigal, whose desire for his share of wealth overcame his obligations to family and community and deceived him into believing that the purpose in life, just as the Gentiles believed, is accumulation and consumption. He became one of them—a Hellenist. If following Jesus matters to us at all, each of us must ask: How close am I to becoming a Hellenist?

THINK ABOUT IT
Where Do We Put Our Trust?

As we've explored, the prodigal left the community of the *beth ab* and went to the "far country" where his pursuit of the lifestyle there led him to squander his inheritance in wild living. During the exodus, God's people also felt the pull of the pagan lifestyle of Egypt—the mad pursuit of wealth and pleasure. God warned his people that this temptation would be difficult to overcome after they settled in the Promised Land. He wanted them to know him, obey him, and trust him to supply their every need. So he tested them during their journey from Egypt to Canaan in order to see if they would love him with all their heart, with all their soul, and with all their strength.

The First Test at Marah (Exodus 15:22–27). Shortly after God miraculously delivered the Hebrews from Pharaoh's army, God "put them to the test," implying that he gave them an opportunity to put their belief into practice so that he could determine whether their commitment was truly real. He wanted them to learn by experience that he did not create them to live on bread alone but on every one of his words.[12]

The Second Test in the Wilderness of Sin and God's Provision of Manna (Exodus 16; Deuteronomy 8:2–3, 14–16; Psalm 78:12–19). God wanted Israel to depend completely on him rather than on themselves as they had in Egypt. He provided only enough manna for each day so that they would have to trust in him (rather than in their own ability to save for the future) to have food for the next day. This is not to say that saving and investing are wrong; God simply desires that we depend on his moment-by-moment provision and not fall into the temptation of depending on our efforts to supply what we need.

Their Future Test (Deuteronomy 6:10–13; 8:6–14, 17–20). God tested Israel three times between the Reed (Red) Sea and Mount Sinai to train them to live on every word that came from his mouth and to trust in him, not in themselves. Moses warned that they'd face more opportunities to demonstrate the faith in their hearts when they became prosperous! Would they remain completely dependent on the Lord when they were so blessed that their own efforts seemed to provide everything they needed?

4. When the younger brother became destitute in the "far country," how was he treated? (See Luke 15:14 – 16.)

What kind of attitude and action toward the destitute did God command his people to display? (See Leviticus 19:10 – 18, 34; Deuteronomy 10:18 – 19; Zechariah 7:10.)

Imagine the pain, grief, and fury of God the Father when any of his lost children are treated as the prodigal was! What do you think we are doing when we, like the pagan world, put our trust in our treasure rather than in God's faithful care and turn our back on the alien and the destitute?

Reflection

When studying this parable in the cultural setting in which Jesus taught it, Western audiences initially resist the idea that a desire for wealth was one of the prodigal's major sins. We seem to find it much easier to identify "sinner" with someone who is sexually immoral, who steals, or who murders. It is much more personal to look in the mirror and recognize our own tendency to be prodigals. But when our possessions, our pursuit after pleasure and leisure, and our need to save up treasure on earth begin to consume us, we have in a sense left the "Father's house."

Money is a resource. We all need it. Money in itself is not bad, but the *love* of money is. The real issue is an issue of heart and mind. That is why Jesus cautioned, "For where your treasure is, there your heart will be also" (Matthew 6:21). Jesus knew all about the seductive power of material wealth and its tendency to distract us from a life of trust and faith. It seems that one indication that money has become our master is whether or not we are stingy with our resources. Prodigals are more common than we tend to think.

In what ways has the seduction of wealth drawn us into what is essentially a pagan lifestyle that seeks contentment in economic possession and consumption?

Think about how often our need for income (to pay bills for what we bought on credit, perhaps) robs our families, churches, and people around us who need what God has provided for us to give to them.

How easy is it to cheat our children of time by trying to earn more, get a promotion, or expand our business because we need more income?

How easy is it for us to pursue material wealth and lose sight of the purpose for which God has redeemed us: to be a royal priesthood that uses its resources to seek out those who are lost and "eat with" them in order to bring *shalom* to the chaos of their lives?

How often does the idolatry of wealth and the pursuits that go with it affect our ability and willingness to have compassion for those in need and to expend ourselves for their benefit?

Memorize

But godliness with contentment is great gain. For we brought nothing into the world, and we can take nothing out of it. But if we have food and clothing, we will be content with that. Those who want to get rich fall into temptation and a trap and into many foolish and harmful desires that plunge people into ruin and destruction.

1 Timothy 6:6 – 9

Day Five | The Prodigal Turns His Thoughts toward Home

The Very Words of God

My sheep wandered over all the mountains and on every high hill. They were scattered over the whole earth, and no one searched or looked for them.... I myself will tend my sheep and have them lie down, declares the Sovereign Lord. I will search for the lost and bring back the strays.

Ezekiel 34:6, 15 – 16

Bible Discovery

The Path Back to the Father's House

For a while, life in the "far country" seemed to suit the lost son. Then tragedy struck. He had no more money. He had lost everything. Because he had lost his family inheritance to the Gentiles, he could not return home. He would be permanently expelled from his community and his father's house. To make matters worse, a famine came to the "far country." He had come to the sad ending of any path that leads away from the Father's house. But it wasn't the end of the story.

Like the lost sheep and the lost coin, the lost son would not be found unless someone searched for him and found him. As odd as it may seem, the famine was the beginning of the prodigal's journey home. God is the one who sends or withholds the rain. Both abundance and famine come from his hand (2 Kings 8:1). God was seeking his lost son!

1. In Luke 15:14 – 16, Jesus shows that the lost son has hit bottom. What is he willing to do, and for what benefit?

There are several nuances we can learn from in this part of the parable:

- The only benefit of the prodigal's work was that he could eat what the pigs ate, most likely the pods of the carob tree. In Jewish tradition, when Israel is so poor they are reduced to eating carob, they will repent and seek the Lord.[13]
- Jesus told this parable in response to criticism that he was eating with "sinners." In a sense he is saying, "Yes, I am. And it is worse than you think; they work for pagans, they live like pagans, and they feed pigs!"
- What a comment Jesus was making on the self-serving worldview of a "far country." The citizen, who is obviously someone of wealth and importance, considers it more important to feed his pigs than to feed a destitute human being.

Jesus had not yet finished the parable, but because what was lost was found in the first two parts, his Jewish audience was probably figuring out that the young man would be found too. But how?

FOR GREATER UNDERSTANDING
The Unforgivable Loss

In the Torah, God instructed that family land (*nahala*) he entrusted to Jewish families in the days of Joshua must remain in the family. If it were lost, he gave commands on how it was to be returned: by the actions of a family member (a kinsman redeemer such as Boaz was for Naomi and Ruth), or if that were not possible, on the fiftieth year—the year of Jubilee (Leviticus 25). Since Gentiles were not bound by the Torah or Jewish cultural customs, families who lost their *nahala* to Gentiles might never get it back. In Jesus' day, many Jewish people lost their land to Roman tax collectors—publicans—and had little hope of getting it back. The Zealot movement that promoted violent resistance to Roman rule was motivated by such loss.

Losing family property to a Gentile was a nearly unforgivable sin in the first century. There was a Jewish custom that any person who lost the family *nahala* and chose to return to the community would be expelled from that community. In a ceremony called *kezazah*—meaning "the cutting off"—someone from the community would break a large pot filled with fruit or grain in front of the offender and the whole community to indicate that the offender was "cut off." From that time no one in the community, not even the family, would have any interaction with that person.[14]

2. The lost son's circumstances were so desperate that he began to make a new plan. Read Luke 15:17 – 20.

   a. What did he realize?

   b. What did he plan to do?

c. How did he propose to overcome the obvious obstacles?

DID YOU KNOW?
Remez Gives a Clue

In ancient times, Jewish sages would choose a word or phrase from the Hebrew Bible and use it in their teaching without referencing it as a quote. Their students, who were well-versed in the Text, would recognize it and bring in the point of the passage from which the reference was quoted. This technique is called *remez* (meaning "hint" or "clue").

In Exodus 10:13–20, Pharaoh said that he had sinned against God and against Moses. But his desire for forgiveness was not repentance; it was only an effort to make the plague of locusts go away. So when the prodigal planned to repeat Pharaoh's words in his "confession" to his father, Jesus' audience would have recognized the source and assumed that the prodigal wasn't repenting, either. The prodigal merely had a scheme to go home and fix his situation.

3. Scholars disagree on whether the son was motivated by repentance at this point or whether his intent was simply to restore his lost resources.

a. What appears to be the son's real concern and goal, and does it reflect repentance?

b. What kind of relationship does he seem to want with his father, and does it reflect a desire for restoration of the relationship?

    c. Whose efforts does the son's plan depend on, and does that reflect the worldview of a "far country" or *beth ab*?

    d. Whose words does the lost son's "confession" reflect, and what does that suggest about the sincerity of his repentance? (See Exodus 10:13 – 20.)

Reflection

The three stories in this parable are Jesus' call to his followers to join him in seeking his lost children. Lost ones — sheep, coins, or sons — do not come back on their own. They may bargain or negotiate, seeming to want the Father's forgiveness for the benefits it offers, but they still want the lifestyle of the "far country." They must be searched for and found if their relationship with the Father is to be restored.

At this point in the parable, Jesus' listeners must have been wondering, *Who will seek the lost?* The answer then — and now — is the same: God will seek them, but his people are his partners and Jesus' parable is an invitation to join him in searching for the lost.

What are we doing to find them?

How willing are we to "eat" with sinners?

How committed are we to being obedient and set apart, yet actively involved in caring for people who are marginalized and outside the Father's house?

Who do you know who is lost, who needs to be found by one of God's "partners"?

THE SEEKING FATHER: THE LOST SON RETURNS

The Hebrew Bible frequently describes God's people as "seeking" the Lord. Sometimes they seek him after they have turned their backs on him and suffered as a result of their disobedience. Others seek the Lord because they know he never forsakes those who seek him. Scripture gives stern warning to those who seek the Lord for their own benefit yet have no compassion for the poor, homeless, and oppressed. Recognizing that the wicked do not seek the Lord, some inspired writers pray for God to act dramatically in order to drive the wicked to seek him. The psalmist, having wandered away, pleads with the Lord who seeks the lost to draw near and find him.

So which is it? Does God seek the lost? Or do the lost seek the Lord? According to the Bible, the answer is "Yes!"

God promises that those who seek him will find him.[1] He also seeks those who are lost and who, like the prodigal in the "far country," seek him in the wrong places. God works in their lives so that in their search they will find that he is near. Jesus' clear message in the parable of the lost son is that the lost are found and safely restored to the father's house because God, the loving Father, seeks them. As one of Jesus' disciples stated, "We love because he first loved us."[2]

The portrayal of God in the final story of Jesus' three-part parable stretches the perspective of many followers of Jesus today. We see that the father is filled with love and compassion for his wandering son, and we relate to him because in some way we, too, have experienced what it's like when someone we love chooses the wrong path.

We might assume that the loving father in this story is Jesus because that is exactly the Savior we have met through the Christian Text. What we don't realize is that the father Jesus described in this parable represents his heavenly Father, the God his listeners knew from the Hebrew Bible!

Although we may struggle to picture the God of the Hebrew Bible as a loving, seeking father, Jesus' audience did not. From the beginning, the Hebrew Bible describes God and his relationship with the people he created using the image of a loving father and a faithful husband.[3] God is the Father who seeks his children who have not simply broken his rules but have broken their relationship with him. He is the Father who would seek his lost son and do anything to bring him back.

Jesus ended this story with a party — a feast — celebrating that the lost had been found. This did not surprise his Middle Eastern audience for whom eating together was a sacred act of friendship and hospitality. Even today, eating together in one's home or tent is an almost sacramental way of engaging with others. It expresses acceptance and support at a very deep level. An invitation to eat with someone is much more than being "friendly," and to reject such an invitation is a great insult. No wonder first century Jews were careful with whom they ate.[4]

Luke's account of this parable (Luke 15) begins with Jewish religious leaders criticizing Jesus for eating with sinners and ends with a feast because one lost sinner was found. Eating with sinners — literally and figuratively — is one way Jesus seeks the lost.

Opening Thoughts (3 minutes)

The Very Words of God

> Seek the LORD while he may be found; call on him while he is near.
>
> **Isaiah 55:6**

Think About It

Most of us have probably experienced a time when we wronged another person deeply enough that we feel uncomfortable, or perhaps even dread, meeting that person face-to-face.

What makes it possible to restore a relationship that is seriously damaged or broken? And how might we go about doing it?

DVD Notes (31 minutes)

The father—always looking for his lost son

Shameless grace that leads to repentance

Make God "near" the lost

How will the parable end?

Sulha: a gift of forgiveness

DVD Discussion (7 minutes)

1. When have you experienced or witnessed grace — the shameless grace the father expressed toward his lost son?

    What impact did that grace have on the people involved in Jesus' story?

    What impact do you think the father's display of grace had on people who heard Jesus' parable — people who took very seriously God's commission to display his reputation to the world so that the lost would come to know him?

What impact does this portrayal of the Father's grace have on you and your understanding of this parable?

2. Let's be honest. When we think of what grace is, do we envision the overwhelming love, unbridled effort, and heart-changing forgiveness that Jesus portrays for us in this parable, or do we see something else? How would you describe grace as you know it?

How would you describe the older brother's understanding of grace?

In what ways do you think our perception of grace affect our efforts to seek those who are lost?

3. Jesus didn't reveal how this story ended. How do you think his listeners, particularly the religious leaders who criticized him in the first place, might have ended it? How would you end it?

DID YOU KNOW?
Jesus in the Decapolis

Locate the following on your map: Galilee, Jerusalem, Sea of Galilee, Nazareth, Qatzrin, Bethsaida, Gamla, Capernaum, Decapolis, Hippos, Tiberias.

Jesus came primarily to seek the lost sheep of Israel, not to evangelize the pagan world around him, although he certainly loved those lost sheep as well. The privilege of seeking the lost in the Gentile world would be left to his disciples and others who came after him. Even though it was not the focus of his ministry, Jesus did not entirely avoid the "far country" known as the Decapolis, which was close to the villages of Galilee where he conducted much of his ministry.

On one occasion Jesus and his disciples crossed the Sea of Galilee to the Decapolis. As soon as they landed on the shore, a man possessed by a legion of demons confronted him (Matthew 8:28–34; Mark 5:1–20; Luke 8:26–39). Jesus cast out the demons and restored *shalom* to the wild,

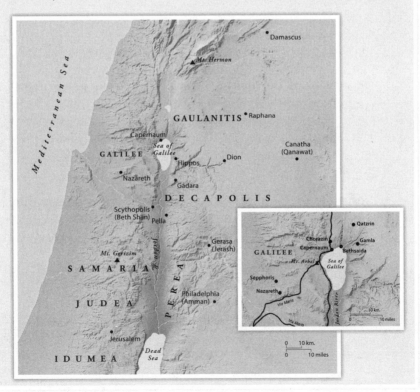

THE DECAPOLIS WAS NOT FAR FROM THE VILLAGES WHERE JESUS LIVED AND TAUGHT. FROM CAPERNAUM A PERSON CAN LOOK ACROSS THE SEA OF GALILEE TO THE EAST AND SEE THE HILLSIDE WHERE THE CITY OF HIPPOS WAS LOCATED. ACROSS THE SEA OF GALILEE TO THE SOUTH IS THE CITY OF TIBERIAS.

tormented man. The man begged to go with Jesus as he was leaving, but Jesus commanded him to return home and tell others what God had done for him. The territory into which Jesus sent him was one of the most challenging mission fields to which he ever called anyone. Later, crowds from the Decapolis sought out and followed Jesus, perhaps a testimony to the effectiveness of the healed man's witness (Mark 7:31 – 36).

Small Group Bible Discovery and Discussion (14 minutes)

The Father Saw Him and Ran!

All of the characters in Jesus' parable about the lost son must have surprised his first-century Galilean audience. None of them acted as one might expect. The younger son asked for his share of the family inheritance, which was a shocking rejection of his Jewish family heritage and an obvious wish for his father's death. The older brother did not exercise his responsibility as the patriarch-in-training to bring reconciliation between his father and brother. He simply took his share of the inheritance, too. Instead of expelling his impertinent son from the family, the father divided the family inheritance and gave it to his sons. But the greatest surprise was yet to come, and it was not the fact that the prodigal returned home. He had few, if any, other options and apparently wanted to regain his financial independence, not to be reconciled to the family.

The most surprising character in this story is the father. His response to his lost son's return is startling, certainly not typical of a first-century Jewish father! His actions make a powerful statement that spiritually lost people are found because their loving Father seeks them. In Jesus' story, we see the Father's grace-filled compassion and love overwhelm his lost son's schemes, lead him to repentance, and draw him back into the "father's house."

1. Luke 15:20 tells us that while the son "was still a long way off, his father saw him and … ran to his son." Given the narrow, winding streets in first-century Galilean villages where it is difficult to see very far in any direction, what must the father have been doing in order to see his son when he was "still a long way off"?[5]

    In this last portion of his three-part parable, Jesus portrays a father whose compassion and love for his lost son is beyond measure. His Jewish audience would have recognized that the father portrays God in the story. What does God's love enable us to do? (See 1 John 4:19.)

    What would love compel a father to do for a lost son?

2. In Jesus' parable, the lost son was seeking something, too. What did he want, and why? (See Luke 15:13 – 19.)

    Do you think the son was seeking a relationship with his father (and by implication in the parable, a relationship with God)? Why or why not?

    As you consider how the son handled his situation, what insight do you gain into why Jesus' parable indicates so strongly that the lost — sheep, coin, or son — will not come back on its own? To what extent do you think the son was capable of seeking God on his own, and what would have happened if no one went to find him?

3. Read Luke 15:17 – 24 again and compare what the son planned to say to his father in Luke 15:17 – 19 with what he actually said in verse 21. What changed in the son's heart, and what happened to his scheme to restore his fortune?

    What do you think the father did that brought his son to true repentance?

What do you realize from this parable about why God wants his people to seek those who are lost in sin?

4. God had other "children" who, much like the prodigal, also journeyed to the "far country," the land of the Gentiles, and nearly perished. What insight do you gain from the following passages into how the lost are found and who ultimately does the seeking? (See Deuteronomy 4:25 – 31; Jeremiah 29:10 – 13; Revelation 3:19 – 20.)

5. What wonderful hope does God offer to those who seek him? (See Psalm 9:10; 145:18; James 4:8.)

DID YOU KNOW?
Old Men Don't Run!

"Traditional Middle Easterners, wearing robes, do not run in public. They never have. To do so would be deeply humiliating."[6] Even today such action would be considered shameful to the old man, the family, and perhaps even the community. While filming this series, we spent time in the camp of a Bedouin family in the desert of Jordan. As we sat together drinking tea in their tent, we talked with the family about whether or not an elderly man would run.

Clearly they had never seen such behavior. The "patriarch" of the family found it humorous even to picture such a thing. Later, he left the tent to check on his flock. As he passed in front of the rolling camera, with a twinkle in his eye, he quickened his step just a bit. It was as if to say, "That's as fast as I will go." We have to wonder if Jesus' audience also chuckled as they imagined such behavior, which they had never seen.

We should note that the father's running wasn't a casual jog. The Greek word Luke chose for "run," *dramon*, is a technical term for the runners in games in the stadium.[7] So the father ran through the village like he was in a race. It is likely that Jesus' audience imagined the entire village following the elderly father after seeing his strange behavior. They knew something was happening!

By using the image of the robed father running, Jesus cleverly connected his parable to other stories in the Hebrew Bible. His hearers would have instantly identified the father with Abraham. Although he was recovering from being circumcised, Abraham ran in the heat of the day to greet three strangers and to bless them through his hospitality. Jesus' listeners also would have remembered how Esau ran to meet his brother Jacob who had deceived him (Genesis 33:4). Esau was willing to humiliate himself in order to be reconciled with Jacob. Jesus' hearers certainly recognized in the younger son's father the same desire for reconciliation.

Faith Lesson (4 minutes)

If we simply think about the younger son's terrible choices and actions, it'd be easy to "write him off" as someone with no positive future. He had ruined his family relationships because of the way he left. He certainly would be shunned by the community he'd insulted. He may even have had such a hard heart that he'd never desire to return to the God he'd disobeyed so grievously. But as we know, the story had a different ending. The lost son had a father who was seeking him and would do anything to restore him to the *beth ab.*

We have to wonder what Jesus' listeners must have thought as he described the father's humiliating run through town to get to his son. Did they understand that Jesus was not only illustrating God's love for each of them but was challenging them to become his agents in seeking the lost, the mission he gave to Israel at Mount Sinai? Did they hear him urging them to be willing to humble themselves — even being humiliated, dishonored, shamed, and laughed at — in order to seek lost prodigals and show them shameless grace?

1. What do we hear and understand Jesus saying to us about seeking the lost?

2. In what ways do we, like those who criticized Jesus for eating with sinners, tend to avoid people who are lost?

3. In what way does this parable challenge our inclination to wait until the lost come crawling to us in remorse and repentance before extending God's grace and love toward them?

4. How do you think Jesus wants us to respond toward those who have offended us, who mock our values and our faith, and who reject our precious Lord?

5. How willing are we, as Jesus' commissioned disciples, to run to modern-day prodigals like the father ran to his son?

Closing (1 minute)

Read Romans 5:6 – 8 aloud together: "You see, at just the right time, when we were still powerless, Christ died for the ungodly. Very rarely will anyone die for a righteous person, though for a good person someone might possibly dare to die. But God demonstrates his own love for us in this: While we were still sinners, Christ died for us."

Then pray, thanking God for the grace and mercy he expresses toward you — and for sending his Son to die for your sins so that you no longer are powerless to them. Thank him for the Messiah's sacrificial death on the cross, through whom all who place their faith in God through Jesus are restored to God's "household." Thank him for loving us so much that he seeks all of his lost children. Ask him to give you an obedient and grace-filled heart for seeking people who are lost, searching for what only he can provide.

Memorize

> *You see, at just the right time, when we were still powerless, Christ died for the ungodly. Very rarely will anyone die for a righteous person, though for a good person someone might possibly dare to die. But God demonstrates his own love for us in this: While we were still sinners, Christ died for us.*
>
> *Romans 5:6 – 8*

Restoring the Lost to the Father's House

In-Depth Personal Study Sessions

Day One | The Father's Grace

The Very Words of God

> *But while he was still a long way off, his father saw him and was filled with compassion for him; he ran to his son, threw his arms around him and kissed him. The son said to him, "Father, I have sinned against heaven and against you. I am no longer worthy to be called your son." But the father said to his servants, "Quick! Bring the best robe and put it on him. Put a ring on his finger and sandals on his feet. Bring the fattened calf and kill it. Let's have a feast and celebrate. For this son of mine was dead and is alive again; he was lost and is found."*
>
> Luke 15:20 – 24

Bible Discovery

A Lost Son Experiences His Father's Grace

The lost son had reached the end of his resources. His time in the "far country" had been a disaster. His share of the family inheritance was gone and no one would help him. He was reduced not only to feeding pigs but to eating what they ate. Facing a hopeless situation, he came up with a plan and headed toward his former home — not to be restored to the *beth ab,* but because he needed help.

The son knew how seriously he'd wronged his family and everyone he knew. He could have imagined every person he met turning away from him — or worse. And what about his father? The son didn't even know if his father would accept his proposal. We can picture him nervously reciting his plan over and over in his mind as he walked toward home. He could not have imagined the reception he would receive from his father.

1. We read in Luke 15:20 that even though the son had chosen a wrong path, his father "was filled with compassion for him," and eagerly "ran to his son, threw his arms around him and kissed him."

   a. Do you think the father had planned this culturally humiliating act? Why or why not?

   b. What does this display of grace reveal about the father's heart for his lost son who had broken their relationship?

   c. How might this act be related to the father's earlier choice to divide the family inheritance — something unheard of in Jesus' time — rather than requiring the severe punishment the Torah spelled out for a rebellious son?

DID YOU KNOW?

The Father Kissed His Son

When Luke wrote that the father "kissed" his son, he used a Greek word that means he kissed his son again and again, which is a custom for Middle Eastern men greeting one another in deep, loving friendship.[8] This, too, must have surprised Jesus' audience. The father's actions are in keeping with cultural practice of that time, but the son had deeply hurt his father and no longer deserved such an expression of love and friendship.

The father's display of love was not private, reserved, or conditional. In front of the entire community, before the son spoke one word, the father declared his love for the unworthy son. Jesus' audience knew that the son would be shocked: "My father still loves me and still wants me back! After all I've done to hurt him and to betray everything he believes in and has taught me, he wants me back!" Instead of the hostile, angry confrontation he expected — and deserved — the son experienced his father's shameless expression of grace, deep devotion, and love.

2. Followers of Jesus today know that he came to earth as the Lamb of God, the atoning sacrifice for the sins of the whole world (1 John 2:2). What we sometimes overlook is that Jesus is also part of the long history of God's people who accepted their role as God's partners in the mission of restoring *shalom* to his broken world. (See John 17:6 – 8, 25 – 26.)[9]

a. What did Jesus make known about the nature and character of God by portraying the father in his parable as being "filled with compassion" for his son?

b. Just as Jesus portrayed the father in this parable as having a forgiving heart, how did Jesus display through his own life God's willingness to forgive the lost? (See Luke 23:32 – 34.)

THINK ABOUT IT

The father in this parable gives us insight into the caring, compassionate, merciful character of God as Jesus wanted him to be known. Jesus portrays a father who — like his Father — is heartbroken by his wayward son's choices but is eager to seek, forgive, and joyously welcome him back into the *beth ab*.

Reflection

Jesus' audience no doubt recognized that the character of the father in the parable of the lost son reflects that of God, because the Lord as father is a central biblical metaphor. God, the Creator of the universe symbolized by the father, loves his children and gives them the freedom to choose to be part of his *beth ab*. There is little he will not do, even today, to seek and forgive his spiritually lost children and bring them home.[10]

We should recognize not only that God is represented in the character of the father but that Jesus put himself into the parable. Jesus is God incarnate — God in the flesh. Like the father in the parable, he too made a humiliating run to seek and to find his lost children. He left the glory of heaven and the praise of hosts of angels to be born in a "stinking" shepherd's cave. He grew up in relative poverty and likely experienced the isolation and rejection of being the son of an unmarried mother. He was mocked by some in the religious community, considered to be crazy by his family, and betrayed by a friend. When he was arrested by the religious establishment and turned over to the Gentiles, even his closest companions abandoned him. Then he was ridiculed, beaten, and crucified naked for the whole world to see. The father in the parable of the prodigal represents this Jesus who became flesh — not to be acclaimed but to be dishonored — so that he could reconcile his lost children to himself.

At some point, we are all prodigals: lost children who have turned our backs, at least for a time, on the Father and his house. All of us need the unbridled grace of Jesus to seek us out and welcome us back into relationship with the Father.

> How deeply have you experienced the "shameless grace" Jesus has displayed on your behalf?

As a recipient of that grace, how do you respond to Jesus' challenges to seek and find the spiritually lost no matter how great the cost?

Who do you know who needs to be found and embraced by the "shameless grace" of Jesus so that he or she will come to know the Father's love and be restored to his *beth ab* — the household of faith?

What holds you back from an all-out effort to reach out to spiritually lost people with God's love and compassion?

DATA FILE

Discovering Our Caring Father

A century after Jesus' time a scholar in the early church named Marcion concluded that the God of the New Testament found in Jesus' teaching was incompatible with the God of the Old Testament. In his view, the God of the Jewish people was jealous, angry, and unforgiving in contrast to the God of compassion, love, and forgiveness whom Jesus proclaimed. Believing that Jesus defeated and replaced the God of the Old Testament, Marcion preached only from the New Testament and believed that all references to the Hebrew

Text were not God's revelation. Many early church fathers strongly disagreed with him, and Marcion was excommunicated from the church around 144 AD.

Nevertheless, Marcion's viewpoint continues to influence Christian thought. Many people believe that while the Old Testament is God's inspired revelation, it is unnecessary for informing the daily walk of Jesus' followers. Some Old Testament stories are filled with violence and judgment that is difficult to understand, but is the God in the Hebrew Bible different from the God represented in Jesus' parable of the lost son? Was Jesus' teaching about the nature of God radically new — even blasphemous — to people of his day? Were they surprised that the father who symbolized God expressed compassion for his lost son?

Consider the God the people of Jesus' day knew from their Bible — the Old Testament — and see why they knew that the prodigal's compassionate, forgiving father represented the God of their Text.

- God created all things and entrusted his human children to care for that creation, but they sinned, bringing chaos into God's creation and breaking their relationship with the Creator (Genesis 1 – 3).
- In the midst of human rebellion against God, he chose Israel, beginning with Abraham, to be the channel through which all nations would be blessed. God chose Israel not as a rejection of other nations but as his instrument for all other nations to come to know him (Genesis 3 – 12).
- God patiently nurtured his people to be a holy people so they could be the channel of his redemption to others:
  - They were to care for the alien and the stranger (Leviticus 25:35).
  - They were to be his kingdom of priests, putting him on display to all nations (Exodus 19:3 – 6).
  - They were not to profane his name (lessen his reputation) but were to make his name known (Leviticus 22:32; 1 Chronicles 16:8).
  - They were to be a light to the nations (Isaiah 42:6; 49:6; 60:1 – 3).
  - The Israelites were to be God's witnesses that he alone was savior (Isaiah 43:10 – 12).
  - Israel was to declare God's praises so the nations would know him (2 Samuel 22:50; Psalm 9:11; 45:17; Isaiah 12:4).

When Israel, like the prodigal in Jesus' story, walked away from the Father's house, God tenderly sought to bring Israel back (Hosea 2:14–15, 23; 11:1–4, 8–9; Jeremiah 3:19–20; 31:20).

God wanted to be known for his love and mercy, and revealed his seven characteristics of love and compassion before he revealed that he also was a God of justice (Exodus 34:5–7).

Surprising as it is to many, the characteristics of the father in Jesus' parable are taken right out of the Hebrew Bible's description of God. His hearers knew that the compassionate father represented God because that is what they read in their Text. God seeks his lost children—Jew and Gentile alike—in order to bring them back into relationship with himself. His love for the lost and his desire to bring them back to himself has been on display from the beginning.

Day Two | "Father, I Have Sinned"

The Very Words of God

> There was a man who had two sons. The younger one said to his father, "Father, give me my share of the estate." So he divided his property between them.
> Not long after that, the younger son got together all he had, set off for a distant country and there squandered his wealth in wild living. After he had spent everything, there was a severe famine in that whole country, and he began to be in need.... When he came to his senses, he said, "How many of my father's hired men have food to spare, and here I am starving to death! I will set out and go back to my father and say to him: Father, I have sinned against heaven and against you. I am no longer worthy to be called your son; make me like one of your hired men." So he got up and went to his father.
>
> *Luke 15:13–14, 17–20*

Bible Discovery

The Prodigal Is Restored

When the lost son headed for home, he was thinking about his one overwhelming need: food. But after the way he left his father, family, and community he couldn't be sure that his father would even speak to him, much less feed him or give him work. And there was the issue of his inheritance. He had lost it — and lost it to Gentiles. In his small, Jewish community that sin was nearly unpardonable.

The *nahala*, the land that God designated for each family when it entered the Promised Land, was intended to be held in stewardship by that family forever. To sell the land was viewed as an act of rebellion against God. If a family somehow lost the land, God's laws prescribed how it eventually could be returned to them. But these laws applied only to the Jewish community. To lose inherited land to the Gentiles was a serious offense because it might never be returned to the family.

The lost son knew that when his community learned he had lost his inheritance, he would be expelled. As noted previously, after Jesus' time, a ceremony called *kezazah* was practiced. In this ceremony, a large pot filled with fruit or grain was broken in the presence of the offender and the whole community signifying that the offender was "cut off" from the community. From that time forward no one in the community, not even the family, would have any interaction with that person.[11] It is not clear whether *kezazah* was widely practiced in Jesus' day, but many scholars believe it was.[12] Even if the ritual was not established by that time, someone who had lost family property to Gentiles would have been shunned.

So the father in this parable would have to act in an extraordinary manner to restore his son to the family before the community expelled him. Jesus certainly held the attention of his audience as he approached the climax of this third parable in the series. Because what had been lost was found in the parables of the lost sheep and lost coin, his listeners knew the son would be found, too. But they could not imagine that the elderly father would run through the village like he was running a race in order to find his lost son and restore him to the family and community.

1. In any other circumstance, the community would have been inclined to mock and disapprove of the father racing through the village. But the father's self-sacrificing demonstration of love for his lost son, his astonishing willingness to take on the shame of his son's bad choices, must have been deeply moving to Jesus' audience. (See Luke 15:20.)

    a. Who do you think the father represented in the minds of Jesus' audience, and what impact might this realization have had on them and their view of how they were to display God to a lost world?

    b. What kind of influence does it appear the father's display of shameless grace had on the younger son's heart and mind?

2. Reread Luke 15:11 – 20. As the son approached home, what sin do you think he thought he had committed against God and his father? Why is this your conclusion?

3. As the parable continues, the father cut short the son's proposal and showered him with more demonstrations of grace and mercy. (See Luke 15:21 – 22.)

    a. What is missing from the son's "prepared speech" and what he actually said to his father, and why is it significant to the story?

b. Why do you think the son accepted his father's offer of restoration rather than trying to fix his problems through his own efforts, as he had planned to do?

4. What do you think the lost son realized from his father's overwhelming expressions of love that led him to change his self-serving plan and come to a place of true repentance?[13]

5. As it is when any lost sinner responds to the grace of God's seeking, what did the father do for the son who could offer his family nothing in return? (See Luke 15:22 – 24.)

DID YOU KNOW?
The Son's Restoration Is Complete

There is much to learn from the celebration of the lost son being found. For the father, there is no second best. There is no hint that "I'll do this for you, but we both know you really don't deserve it." The father's forgiveness and grace covered every offense. Immediately the father instructed his servants to bring the "best robe," put a ring on the son's finger, and sandals on his feet. Scholars have suggested that the ring was a signet ring, the official family seal, which indicated the prodigal resumed his place as a son. The same would be true of the sandals; at that time children wore shoes while slaves went barefoot.[14] Clearly the father embraced the lost son as a full member of his family.

Reflection

The son discovered that his sin was not losing the family property but breaking his relationship with his father. He could not make up for what he had done. His father made up for it all by seeking him and loving him unconditionally, even at the expense of his own humiliation and shame. Like the lost sheep and coin, the son was found solely because of the efforts of the seeker. The younger son accepted his father's grace and repented when he realized how much his father loved him. That was what Jesus wanted both the Pharisees and the sinners he sat down to eat with to realize: He would do anything to welcome them home.

> In what ways has your study of the parable of the lost sheep, coin, and son helped you to realize that God's sacrificial love that restores you to relationship with him is truly a gift — something you cannot gain for yourself, something you can have only because God by his grace enables you to have it?

> How has God expressed his love and grace toward you, and what impact did his love have on you?

> As a beneficiary of God's shameless grace, as one who has been restored to the *beth ab,* what might need to change in your heart and life so that you will truly display God's grace to his lost children?

What makes it difficult for us (as it apparently was for the Pharisees) to share God's shameless grace with his lost children?

How high a price are you willing to pay to share God's gift of grace with those who are spiritually lost?

Memorize

As for you, you were dead in your transgressions and sins, in which you used to live when you followed the ways of this world and of the ruler of the kingdom of the air, the spirit who is now at work in those who are disobedient. All of us also lived among them at one time, gratifying the cravings of our flesh and following its desires and thoughts. Like the rest, we were by nature deserving of wrath. But because of his great love for us, God, who is rich in mercy, made us alive with Christ even when we were dead in transgressions — it is by grace you have been saved. And God raised us up with Christ and seated us with him in the heavenly realms in Christ Jesus, in order that in the coming ages he might show the incomparable riches of his grace, expressed in his kindness to us in Christ Jesus. For it is by grace you have been saved, through faith — and this is not from yourselves, it is the gift of God — not by works, so that no one can boast.

Ephesians 2:1 – 9

Day Three | The Father Extends His Grace Again

The Very Words of God

> *Meanwhile, the older son was in the field. When he came near the*
> *house, he heard music and dancing. So he called one of the servants*
> *and asked him what was going on. "Your brother has come," he replied,*
> *"and your father has killed the fattened calf because he has him back*
> *safe and sound." The older brother became angry and refused to go in.*
> *So his father went out and pleaded with him.*

Luke 15:25 – 28

Bible Discovery

Another Son Is "Lost"

Often it seems that readers of Jesus' three-part parable give the
younger son most of the attention. But the older son's response to his
father's grace is no less significant. He returned from a day of hard
work in the fields to the sounds of celebration. When he learned that
his younger brother had returned home and his father was celebrating
his restoration to the family, the older brother was not pleased.[15]

1. As soon as the older son discovered what all the excitement
    was about, how did he respond? (See Luke 15:25 – 28.)

2. When the father learned that his older son refused to join the
    celebration, he could have become angry, demanded that his
    older son attend the banquet, expelled his son for his insolence,
    or worse.[16] Instead, what did the father do, willingly and hum-
    bly, that again humiliated him in front of the whole community
    and his recently restored son? (See Luke 15:28 – 32.)

What does the father's response to the older son — another expression of his shameless grace — reveal about the depth of his love for both sons?

What impact did the father's expression of love and grace have on the older son? (See Luke 15:29 – 30.)

How might the older son's response have reflected an attitude similar to what the Pharisees expressed toward the "sinners" with whom Jesus ate?

Would you say the older son had a right to feel this way? Why or why not?

FOR GREATER UNDERSTANDING
What Do We Know About the Older Son?

Although the older son, as the future family patriarch, would have been expected to step in and prevent his father from dividing the family estate between his sons, Jesus did not portray him that way. The older son seems to have been content to receive his "share" as well. He raised no objection until his father welcomed back his prodigal brother. Then he criticized his father for eating with a sinner, which is exactly why the Pharisees criticized Jesus.

Given the culture of Jesus' world, some scholars believe the older son may have worried that his father's acceptance of his younger brother would dishonor the village. If so, Jesus was apparently asking the Pharisees if they resented him welcoming sinners because they might dishonor the "Father"—the Lord. Others have attributed his anger to the loss of the part of "his" estate that funded the celebration, which included not only the fattened calf[17] but quite likely food for the entire community![18] This perspective also seems to fit the older brother's character. Or, he may have just been extremely resentful that his father accepted his brother back into the *beth ab*.

Whatever his reason, the older son greatly humiliated his merciful father by refusing to take his appropriate role in assisting with the celebration. Even this did not diminish his father's love for him. His father responded to his anger by commending his years of faithful service and reaffirming his deep love for him. He then asked him to share in the joy of his brother's restoration to the family. The father had lost a son before; he didn't want to lose another. Jesus ended his parable without telling us if the older brother changed his mind.

3. Whereas the younger son accepted his father's grace and repented, his older brother responded to his father's selfless love differently. What do the older son's words reveal about his heart, including his willingness or unwillingness ...

    • to accept his brother back as a brother?

    • to seek the lost as his father had demonstrated?

    • to forgive his already forgiven brother?

    • to humiliate his father — and his act of grace — even further?

    • to honor the bonds of love that should exist between father and son?

    • to realize that although he had played the role of the obedient son, he also broke a relationship — and his father's heart in the process.

- to imitate the character of his father as patriarch, and cultivate his deepest loyalties to God and his family?

4. The question is: For what reason had the older son remained faithful to his father through the years? (See Luke 15:28–31.)

   a. Whereas the younger brother's lust for the pleasures of wealth became obvious and bore fruit that was terribly destructive, which similar sin(s) did the older brother cultivate in his heart while appearing to work faithfully for his father?

   b. What was the older son's true motivation for all that he did?

   c. What destructive "fruit" did the older brother's sin bear?

Reflection

In Jesus' parable, the younger son indulged in the excesses of the Gentile world and ended up being found — redeemed — by the love and grace of his father. Once lost and dead in sinfulness, he was found and restored to life in the *beth ab*.

The older son — the "good" boy — appeared to be just fine on the outside, but was filled with deceit, selfishness, and resentment. He, too, was dead in sin — consumed by his selfish desire for the material possessions of his father. He was faithful, but not because he loved his father, and certainly not because he loved his lost brother.

Just as the father did not give up on his younger son, he didn't give up on his older son. He expended shameless grace on each one. Certainly the Pharisees understood that Jesus was asking them to welcome sinners the way he did. The question for us is, will we do the same?

> What might we learn from the father that will help us to humbly extend grace to lost people?

> In what way is the relationship between the father and his oldest son a challenge for those of us who claim to follow Jesus to …
>
> • examine our motivation for obeying God? Do we really serve him because we love him with all our heart, all our soul, and all our strength, or do we serve because of the benefits we want to receive from him?

> • examine our faithfulness in accepting his invitation to join him in the mission of seeking the lost? Do we truly welcome lost sinners into God's family, or are there some we would prefer to judge and send away?

- test the authenticity of our love for the lost? Are we willing to sacrifice our pride and extend love in ways that may humiliate us just for the opportunity to say, on behalf of Jesus our Lord, "I love you, and I want you to be restored to my family"?

Day Four | Celebrating the Return of Shalom

The Very Words of God

> *"My son," the father said, "you are always with me, and everything I have is yours. But we had to celebrate and be glad, because this brother of yours was dead and is alive again; he was lost and is found."*

> *Luke 15:31 – 32*

Bible Discovery

The Father Celebrates a Lost Son's Reconciliation

For millennia, tribes, families, and individuals in Middle Eastern cultures have shared ceremonial meals together as a sign of resolved conflict, forgiveness, mutual respect, acceptance, peace, and friendship. When a new covenant is forged, it is confirmed by a shared meal. When people experience conflict, they seek reconciliation by rituals that include a shared friendship meal. When parties covenant to not take vengeance on each other, they sit down to a ceremonial meal to celebrate their reconciliation. After the meal, neither party will bring up any past offenses again.

The Bible records many examples of peace, harmony, and goodwill expressed through a ceremonial meal. Abraham and Sarah prepared a feast to welcome three strangers and unknowingly shared a meal with the Lord and two angels. God established feasts like Passover to commemorate his redemption of Israel and to celebrate the covenant relationship that resulted. And Jesus often attended a feast or talked about a feast to come. Some of his most profound teaching came at the last feast of Passover he shared with his disciples. So it was no surprise that Jesus ended each part of his parable about the lost sheep, coin, and son with a feast celebrating that the lost was found.

FOR GREATER UNDERSTANDING
Covenant Meals in a Biblical Context[19]

When Adam and Eve sinned and broke their covenant relationship with God, all of humanity became alienated from him. But God was determined to restore sinful people to intimate relationship with him. So he entered into a redemptive covenant of faith first with Abraham and eventually, through his descendants, with all people who submit to him as Lord.

Throughout the history of his redemptive work, God has restored covenant fellowship through sacrifice (Psalm 50:4–5). Consistent with Middle Eastern custom, the restored relationship was celebrated and experienced by eating a friendship meal. Over time the meals God's people practiced came to anticipate the Messiah's final banquet when God will dwell with his people in the New Jerusalem. The various covenant meals described in the Bible provide the context for the Passover that Jesus used to create the covenant meal his followers continue to celebrate to "remember" him (1 Corinthians 11:24–25).

One kind of fellowship meal—the reconciliation meal today called *sulha* in Arabic[20]—is still used to restore relationship between people who have been wronged. During this ceremonial meal, the offended parties sit down together. After making a solemn covenant not to seek vengeance for wrongs suffered, they break bread. By eating together, they celebrate their reconciliation and afterward neither party will ever bring up the grievance again.

The psalmist referred to such a meal when he praised the Lord his shepherd and said, "You prepare a table before me in the presence of my enemies" (Psalm 23:5). From a Western cultural view one might think David was celebrating the fact that God spread a table for him and was protecting him from enemies who watched his feasting. But from a Middle Eastern view, God had prepared a *sulha*—where David sat with his enemies and as they broke bread they were reconciled and became friends.

1. After God delivered the Hebrews from slavery in Egypt, he brought them to himself at Mount Sinai (Exodus 24). There, in an amazing demonstration of his love, God established an intimate covenant with Israel that is best described as a marriage.[21]

   a. What did God's people then do to "consummate" the covenant? (See Exodus 24:3 – 8.)

   b. After the people professed their desire to be in relationship with God, what did Moses and the elders of Israel do, at God's invitation, on behalf of all of the people? (See Exodus 24:9 – 11.)

2. The fellowship offerings (sometimes translated "peace") take their name from the Hebrew word *shalom*. They were a significant element of the sacrificial system God established to remove the guilt of Israel's sin. Of the four major sacrifices (burnt offering, sin, guilt, and peace), the peace sacrifice was the only one in which the worshiper is allowed to eat part of the sacrifice. The *shalom* established by the sacrifice was confirmed, demonstrated, and celebrated through a covenant meal that also included bread and drink. Everyone — the Lord (Leviticus 3:3 – 4), the priest (Leviticus 7:34), and the worshiper — shared in this meal. (See Leviticus 3:1 – 17; 7:11 – 38.)

   a. At Mount Sinai, the people sacrificed their fellowship offerings, and God shared a fellowship meal with his "bride" (the seventy elders of Israel) to confirm the friendship that now existed between them! The implications of this certainly stunned these ancient people. How do you think remembering the origin of these sacrifices would affect your experience of God when you brought an animal to sacrifice at the temple, burning the best portions as an offering to the Lord and then eating the meat with the priest?

b. Why do you think God established this meal — a full covenant communion with him as if he were present at the table with them as they ate?

3. Fellowship meals occurred several times annually during the great festivals God's ancient people held to celebrate and promote awareness of God's faithfulness and love. As you consider the examples of fellowship offerings and meals found in the following Scripture passages, what insight do you gain into how they experienced their relationship with God? (See Joshua 4:19 – 23; 5:2 – 12; 1 Kings 8:62 – 66; 2 Chronicles 30:1 – 27.)

4. Read Isaiah 25:6 – 9 and Revelation 21:3 – 4. When *shalom* is fully restored, where will God dwell, and who will be invited to share in an amazing covenant meal with him?

5. Jesus participated in many fellowship meals with sinners, tax collectors, and his disciples. When it was time for him to

establish a covenant meal to remember his redemptive work, he chose the Passover — a meal of reconciliation because he was God's "lamb" sacrificed for us, and a meal of fellowship because those who follow him are fully restored members of his *beth ab*. Since the meal confirms and portrays that those who follow Jesus are reconciled to and in fellowship with God as his family, why must we be reconciled with each other as we eat his meal together — having no bitterness or divisions among us? (See Luke 22:14 - 20 and also Romans 12:4 - 5; 1 Corinthians 10:16 - 17; 11:17 - 29; 12:12 - 27.)

6. Genesis 31:22 - 55 chronicles Jacob's conflict with his mother's brother, Laban. What did they eventually do to seal the covenant they made to not harm each other and to confirm their reconciliation?

THINK ABOUT IT

Jesus Prepares a Sulha for Peter

After his resurrection, Jesus prepared a *sulha* or reconciliation meal to restore Peter to his place after he had denied Jesus on the night he was arrested (John 18:15 – 27). Notice the similarity to the story of the prodigal son. First, Peter publicly rejected Jesus in the most hurtful way; then he may have even decided to give up being a disciple and return to his fishing trade.[22] Like the prodigal's father, Jesus — the offended person — went to look for Peter. Jesus prepared food, spoke to Peter about the break in their relationship, and then reinstated him as his disciple (John 21:1 – 19). This took on the character of a meal of reconciliation.

7. Let's go back to Jesus' parable of the lost sheep, coin, and son. Immediately after the lost son's repentance, what did his father do? (See Luke 15:21 – 24.)

In light of the previous two parables that Jesus told, who was being celebrated and why? (Note: "He was lost *and* is found" from v. 24.)

In light of the Middle Eastern custom of reconciliation and friendship meals, why would it have been important for everyone in the family and community to share in this celebration?

For what reasons was the older brother's refusal to participate such a great offense? (See Luke 15:31 – 32.)

Reflection

An Israeli Christian, Ilan Zamir, unintentionally killed an Arab family's deaf thirteen-year-old son in a car accident. Afterward he wanted to seek forgiveness from the boy's family. Many people tried to stop him; the Arab culture allows family members to kill in revenge for a son's death. But he insisted, so an Arab pastor helped him to arrange a *sulha*. During this meal, Zamir apologized and offered gifts for what he had done. The family would not accept these gifts. But when the father of the dead boy began the meal he demonstrated to everyone his forgiveness. The family then said to Zamir, "Know, O my brother, that you are in place of this son who has died. You have a family and a home somewhere else, but know that here is your second home."[23] What a miracle of grace and mercy!

When the prodigal son in Jesus' parable returned and repented as a result of his father's grace, the father arranged a feast to celebrate that his son was restored to the family by his father's sacrificial action. The feast celebrated the father's finding and receiving of his son and the fact the son was fully restored. In that sense, the feast is a *sulha* — a meal of reconciliation. Jesus' hearers knew that when the meal was over no one would speak again of the son's hurtful, sinful actions.

In light of the *sulha* and the fellowship meals, why must those of us who follow Jesus live every moment of every day in close fellowship with the God to whom we are reconciled?

To what extent do we actually celebrate our relationship with Messiah Jesus?

Is there someone you know with whom you need to share a *sulha* and move beyond your grievances into a reconciled relationship as friends? If so, how will you proceed?

Who might you invite, today, to a fellowship meal in your home?

Memorize

You prepare a table before me in the presence of my enemies. You anoint my head with oil; my cup overflows. Surely your goodness and love will follow me all the days of my life, and I will dwell in the house of the LORD *forever.*

Psalm 23:5 – 6

Day Five | How Does the Parable End?

The Very Words of God

My prayer is not for them alone. I pray also for those who will believe in me through their message, that all of them may be one, Father, just as you are in me and I am in you. May they also be in us so that the world may believe that you have sent me. I have given them the glory that you gave me, that they may be one as we are one — I in them and you in me — so that they may be brought to complete unity. Then the world will know that you sent me and have loved them even as you have loved me.

John 17:20 – 23

Bible Discovery

Living in Unity to Reach the Lost

Jesus' story about the prodigal son is sad in part because the family is broken and dysfunctional. It is not the strong, supportive, extended family community God intended the *beth ab* to be.[24] The father's willingness to humiliate himself and express shameless grace brought his son, who had been lost to the pleasures and materialism of the Gentile world, to repentance and restoration. But the elder brother, who apparently viewed his father as merely a means to achieve his own financial gain, took a harsh, judgmental stance toward his brother. The father begged his elder son to also show grace and celebrate the restoration of his brother to the family (Luke 15:31 – 32).

And that is where Jesus ended his story. He never revealed whether the older brother continued his bitter rejection of his brother and his father's grace or whether he accepted both and rejoiced in the restoration of the family. Why didn't he end the story?

Remember, this parable was Jesus' response to the Pharisees' concern about his association with "unclean" sinners. It was his plea for them to join him in seeking those who are lost so that they would be restored to the Father's house. He wanted them to know that love and grace can lead the dirtiest, hardest heart to repentance. This parable speaks powerfully to Jesus followers today. Like the Pharisees, we are called to be God's kingdom of priests who display his character and grace to the lost so that they, too, will be restored to the Father's house.

1. The concern Jesus showed for those whose lives were in chaos — even the chaos their own sin had created — is consistent and amazing. He interacted with the unclean — sinners, tax collectors, lepers, and others to whom he expressed grace and compassion. Yet he was sinless, never approving of their sin. He walked the balance between compassionate involvement in the lives of those who were broken by sin and resisting even the appearance of evil. And he instructed his disciples to do the same. In light of 1 John 2:6, what is the responsibility of those who follow Jesus to seek and find people who are spiritually lost?

2. It has always been a challenge for God's people to walk the
    "tightrope" between being holy people of God who remain
    separate from sin *and* being people who get out and engage
    the world in order to seek and find the lost. Take time to
    thoughtfully review the following Bible passages. Note how
    each one instructs us in finding the balance between the
    need to be set apart from sin and the need for compassionate
    interaction with those who are spiritually lost.

The Text	How We Balance Holiness with Compassionate Involvement
Ex. 19:4–6	
Ezek. 20:32–41	
Ps. 105:1	
Matt. 5:14–16	
Matt. 8:2–3	
Mark 7:31–37	
Luke 15:1–2	
2 Cor. 6:14–18	

3. Jesus' parable also encourages God's people who live in a
    culture that doesn't share our beliefs or values to be a uni-
    fied community. It is important that we be joined by a com-
    mon desire to do whatever it takes to display God's love and
    grace to sinners so that they can be restored to the Father's
    house. What do you learn about being a united community
    of priests who display God's character and love from the fol-
    lowing? (See John 13:34–35; Romans 12:10–18; Ephesians
    4:1–3; Hebrews 10:24.)

Reflection

God desires that everyone who claims to follow Jesus display his character and nature to a broken world without becoming like those who do not know him. Jesus modeled such a balance, resisting even the appearance of evil and yet being compassionately involved with people whose lives were in chaos from sin. His three-part parable was an open invitation for the Pharisees — who wanted to obey God — to join him in seeking and restoring the lost to the Father's house. How would they see themselves in the parable and respond? Would they do what Jesus taught and modeled for them?

The same question stands for those who seek to follow Jesus today. How do we see ourselves in this parable?

> Each of us at one time — like the sheep, the coin, and the son — was lost. Are there ways in which we are still rejecting the Father? Are we living in the "far country" of ungodly attitudes or actions? Have we allowed our desire for wealth and pleasure to override our willingness to seek the lost?

> Are we — like the shepherd, the woman, and the father — people who love the lost and will stop at nothing to bring them back? Jesus' display of shameless grace brought many to repentance. Will we increase his reputation by displaying the same compassion and grace he has shown to us?

Or are we like the older brother, living in the Father's house because of what it provides us? Do we find great joy in the grace that brings a lost child of God to repentance and restoration, or do we resent and reject the sinner?

What will we do through the power and wisdom of God ...

- to stand before the world and display him consistently and lovingly so that spiritually lost people can be restored to the Father's house?

- to display "shameless grace" to a prodigal we know — a child, grandchild, sibling, friend, or even a parent — and partner with God in bringing this lost child of God to repentance?

- to encourage one another to seek the lost — and also remain holy?

Memorize

Therefore, if anyone is in Christ, the new creation has come: The old has gone, the new is here! All this is from God, who reconciled us to himself through Christ and gave us the ministry of reconciliation: that God was reconciling the world to himself in Christ, not counting people's sins against them. And he has committed to us the message of reconciliation. We are therefore Christ's ambassadors, as though God were making his appeal through us. We implore you on Christ's behalf: Be reconciled to God.

2 Corinthians 5:17 – 20

NOTES

Introduction

1. Exodus 6:7; 7:5; 8:10; 9:29; 14:4.

2. Genesis 1:28; 2:15.

3. Genesis 12:1 – 4.

4. Exodus 19:3 – 6.

5. 1 Peter 2:11 – 12.

6. 1 Peter 2:9.

7. Sandra L. Richter, *The Epic of Eden* (Downers Grove, Ill.: IVP Academic, 2008), chapter 1. See also Kenneth E. Bailey, *Jacob and the Prodigal* (Downers Grove, Ill.: IVP Academic, 2003), chapter 1, sections 1 and 3. These provide an excellent description of the need to understand and the proper use of the cultural setting of the Bible.

8. See Acts 1:1 – 2. Jesus "began" to do and to teach in his earthly ministry. Certainly Jesus' work continues in and through his followers, his disciples.

9. Genesis 6 – 7.

10. Genesis 18 – 19.

11. Genesis 23:6 (ESV).

12. Jonathan Sacks, in a speech entitled "The Western World and the Judaeo-Christian Revelation of God," presents a powerful vision of God working through his people who have little power or influence on their own. I find this idea compelling, given how tempting it is to seek to bring about God's will by economic or political power alone rather than by faithful living.

Session 1: Abraham and Sarah and Three Strangers

1. Christopher J. H. Wright, *The Mission of God* (Downers Grove, Ill.: IVP Academic, 2006), 279.

2. Tamar (Genesis 38), those who joined the exodus (Exodus 12:37–38), and Rahab the Canaanite prostitute (Joshua 2) were redeemed into God's people before Ruth. The great theme of God using his people, like Boaz, to display him so that others will join in God's plan for redemption is continued in Jesus' mission to his disciples — and through them, to us.

Session 2: Israel at Sinai: The First Great Commission

1. For a more complete study of what God intended by bringing his people out of bondage in Egypt, meeting with them at Mount Sinai, and leading them into the Promised Land, please see That the World May Know, Vol. 8, God Heard *their Cry*; Vol. 9, Fire on the Mountain; and Vol. 10, With All Your Heart.

2. Two suggestions as a beginning point are James K. Hoffmeier's *Ancient Israel in Sinai* (New York: Oxford University Press, 2011), and Barry Beitzel's *Moody Atlas of the Bible* (Chicago: Moody Press, 1985). These authors present the alternatives, taking the biblical text as a historically accurate source. They have a point of view, both supporting something close to the traditional location, but present evidence for other opinions as well. Their bibliographic references provide a place to begin considering all major theories.

3. For further study of covenants in God's relationship with his people, see That the World May Know, Vol. 2, *Prophets and Kings,* 165–197.

4. See Ecclesiastes 2:8 and 1 Chronicles 29:3, where *segulah* is used in the Hebrew text.

5. In order to more fully understand the role of the tabernacle (and later the temple) in God's redemptive plan, please refer to sessions 1 and 2 of That the World May Know, Vol. 10, *With All Your Heart.*

6. www.rabbisacks.org/covenant-conversation-tetsaveh-prophet-and-priest/...

7. Jon D. Levenson, *Sinai and Zion* (San Francisco: HarperOne, 1987). In the chapter entitled "Ethics, Ritual and Covenant Theology," Levenson gives an excellent summary of the Jewish idea of the imitation of God. One will clearly see the roots of the New Testament teaching of the imitation of Jesus.

8. See En-Gedi Resource Center at www.egrc.net, "Directors Article," June 2003, and "Biblical Dress: Tassels." See also Jacob Milgram, "Excursus 38 on Tassels (*Tsitsit*)," the *Jewish Publication Society Commentary on Numbers*, 1990.

9. For more information regarding tassels, please see That the World May Know, Vol. 3, *Life and Ministry of the Messiah*, Session 5.

10. Luke 24:50. At his ascension Jesus "lifted up his hands and blessed them." This blessing with raised arms was a priestly act in the first century. It may be that Luke is pointing toward Jesus and his priestly role. This idea is strengthened by the fact that Luke begins his account with a righteous priest who loses his voice because of a lack of faith in God's provision and cannot give the blessing that normally would follow (Luke 1:20 – 22). Where the human priest ultimately failed, Jesus the greater priest was faithful.

11. www.rabbisacks.org/a-judaism-engaged-with-the-world/.

12. Ibid., 14.

13. Ibid., 16.

14. Ibid., 27.

Session 3: Jesus Renews the Mission: Seeking the Lost

1. Steven Fine and Ann Killebrew, "Qatzrin — Reconstructing Village Life in Talmudic Times," *Biblical Archaeology Review* (May/June 1991), 44 – 56.

2. Taanit 14b, Megilla 5b.

3. I am indebted to Ken Bailey for this lesson. He has written extensively on this subject and is an ordained Presbyterian minister, a well-respected New Testament scholar, teacher, and author. He has taught at seminaries and institutes in Egypt, Lebanon, Jerusalem, and Cyprus as well as Pittsburgh and McCormick Presbyterian Seminaries and Fuller Theological Seminary.

4. Bailey, *Jacob and the Prodigal*, chapter 6. Bailey presents the cultural setting of this parable in a most insightful way.

5. Brad H. Young, *The Parables: Jewish Tradition and Christian Interpretation* (Peabody, Mass.: Hendrickson, 1998), Chapter 10.

6. Kenneth E. Bailey, *The Cross and the Prodigal: The 15th Chapter of Luke, Seen Through the Eyes of Middle Eastern Peasants* (St. Louis: Concordia, 1973), 29. Bailey also notes that this was the issue between Peter and Paul regarding eating with Gentiles. The question was not about having a conversation, being at the same table, or eating the same food. It was about accepting Gentiles as part of one's community at the deepest level.

7. See Nehemiah 8. Ezra the priest led the Jewish community. Clearly the Torah now played a more central role in Jewish life than it had earlier.

8. *Tanakh* is the Hebrew term for the Hebrew Bible, made up of letters from the words for the three parts of Tanakh: T from Torah (meaning "instruction") that includes the first five books; N from *Nevi'im* for the "Prophets" that includes the history and prophetic books; and *Ketuvim* for the Writings. See Luke 24:44, where Jesus used a similar grouping of the Scriptures.

9. To explore in more depth the topics of the "Lord is my shepherd" and shepherding, study related material in That the World May Know, Vol. 2, *Prophets and Kings*, Session 5; Vol. 10, *With All Your Heart*, Session 3; and Vol. 12, *Walking with God in the Desert*, Session 6.

10. Bailey, *Jacob and the Prodigal*, Chapter 7.

11. Ibid.

12. Bailey, *Jacob and the Prodigal*, Chapter 8. Bailey presents an excellent survey of Jesus' way of including all of his community in his teaching.

13. See also Acts 22:3.

14. Bailey, *The Cross and the Prodigal*, 35.

15. Bailey, *Jacob and the Prodigal* and *The Cross and the Prodigal*. Also Young, *The Parables: Jewish Tradition and Christian Interpretation*. I am particularly indebted to the work of these two scholars and highly recommend their treatment of this parable because they have shaped my understanding of Jesus' teaching. Chapter 7 of Young's book presents an outstanding study of the parable of the lost son in light of its Jewish context.

16. Young, *The Parables: Jewish Tradition and Christian Interpretation*, 140.

17. Kenneth Bailey notes that Luke uses "inheritance" elsewhere, but here uses a word translated as "estate." Inheritance would imply the son's acceptance of responsibility to provide for family members' needs and to act in their best interest — of which he apparently wanted no part.

18. Kenneth E. Bailey, *Poet and Peasant and Through Peasant Eyes* (Grand Rapids: Wm. B. Eerdmans, 1983). The idea of asking this question of several Arab families with whom I am acquainted came from Bailey's account of his own experiences.

19. Ibid., 169. Reconciliation in the Middle East is always brought about by a third party, and the eldest son would be expected to take the role of reconciler.

Session 4: The Lost Son: In a Far Country

1. Deuteronomy 4:5 – 8; 1 Chronicles 16:8; Isaiah 42:6.

2. 1 John 2:6.

3. Young, *The Parables: Jewish Tradition and Christian Interpretation*, Chapter 7.

4. Scholars estimate there are more than four thousand extant parables from ancient times, including those of Jesus. There are varying opinions as to which of Jesus' lessons are actually parables. Some people believe his teaching concerning the vine (John 15) and the good shepherd (John 10) are parables; others disagree. Based on my study of parables in the Jewish context, I think about 60 parables of Jesus are included in the Gospels. Scholars' estimates range from 35 to 65. Whatever the number actually was (assuming he told many more parables not recorded in the Gospels; see Matthew 13:34–35), this technique was very important in his teaching style.

5. Luke 20:19.

6. I am indebted to Ken Bailey for this lesson.

7. Bailey, *The Cross and the Prodigal*, 53.

8. See Genesis 3:1–7. The original temptation and sin involved our ancestors doing what seemed right and good for them, putting them on God's level or above — as suggested by Satan, whose kingdom is based on putting oneself ahead of the Creator.

9. Leo Dupree Sandgren, *The Shadow of God* (Peabody, Mass.: Hendrickson, 2003). Chapter 14, titled "The Power of the Name," is a fictional account of the Romans' use of their gods' names and their desire to know the name of the God of the Jews. For an account of a first-century story written by Jewish philosopher Philo, in which Roman Emperor Caligula tries to trick Philo into pronouncing God's name, see the chapter titled "The Embassy."

10. Bailey, *The Cross and the Prodigal*, 53–54.

11. Ibid., 53.

12. Deuteronomy 8:2–3. Read James 1:2–4, 12, where James described the value of God's testing, providing an opportunity to put into practice what is believed even when times

are difficult because it provides discipline and training for his people.

13. Young, *The Parables: Jewish Tradition and Christian Interpretation*, 145.

14. Bailey, *The Cross and the Prodigal*, 52.

Session 5: The Seeking Father: The Lost Son Returns

1. Proverbs 8:17; Jeremiah 29:13.

2. 1 John 4:19.

3. Jeremiah 3:19–20.

4. Galatians 2:11–13; see also Acts 10:27–29. This was the issue in the early church as well.

5. Bailey, *Jacob and the Prodigal*, Chapter 9.

6. Ibid, 109. See also Bailey's treatment of this subject in *Finding the Lost: Cultural Keys to Luke 15*, (St. Louis: Concordia, 1992); Bailey, *Poet and Peasant and Through Peasant Eyes*, Chapter 6.

7. Bailey, *The Cross and the Prodigal*, 67.

8. Ibid, 68.

9. Jesus says literally, "I have made your *name* known" (John 17:26). In that world, your name was your character, your reputation, who you were. To make someone's name known is to increase his or her reputation or honor.

10. Young, *The Parables: Jewish Tradition and Christian Interpretation*, Chapter 7.

11. Bailey, *The Cross and the Prodigal*, 52.

12. Bailey, *Poet and Peasant and Through Peasant Eyes*, 167ff. Bailey, *Jacob and the Prodigal*, 102. See also "Kezazah," *Encyclopedia Judaica* (Jerusalem: Ketar Publishing). Bailey also notes a reference in the Dead Sea Scrolls from Jesus' day, warning about the loss of the inherited property to Gentiles (Ibid., 102).

13. Bailey, *Poet and Peasant and Through Peasant Eyes*, 180ff.

14. See *The NIV Study Bible* (Grand Rapids: Zondervan, 1985), 1570.

15. Bailey, *Poet and Peasant and Through Peasant Eyes*. See pp. 192ff for an excellent study of the older son.

16. Deuteronomy 21:18 – 21. Although stoning was extremely rare in the first century, the Torah did provide that punishment for a rebellious son. This was a serious offense against the father, who could have insisted that his son be stoned publicly. Instead, he pleads with him to return.

17. See 1 Samuel 28:24; Amos 6:4.

18. Bailey, *Poet and Peasant and Through Peasant Eyes*, 186ff.

19. I am greatly indebted to Lois Tverberg for her work explaining ancient meal customs. See Ann Spangler and Lois Tverberg, *Sitting at the Feet of Rabbi Jesus* (Grand Rapids: Zondervan, 2009), Chapter 10.

20. *Sulha* is the Arabic equivalent of the Hebrew word *shulhan* meaning "table." The use of the word for the meal of reconciliation stems from the hospitality of the Middle East in which eating at the same table is the essence of *shalom,* or friendship and harmony between people.

21. In Jeremiah 2:1, Hosea 2:14 – 19, and Exodus 6:7, God promises to "take" Israel as his people — a verb used in the Torah for marriage. Isaac "took" Rebecca, and she became his wife (Genesis 24:67).

22. Mark 16:7. The instructions given are "go tell the disciples *and Peter"* [emphasis added], implying Peter was no longer one of the disciples. This may help to explain why he was fishing when Jesus restored him.

23. To purchase a copy of this amazing story, go to: store.jew forjesus.org/the-sulha-reconciliation-in-the-middle-east.html.

24. See David Daube, *Inheritance*, as quoted by Kenneth E. Bailey in *Poet and Peasant and Through Peasant Eyes*, 169.

ACKNOWLEDGMENTS

The production of this study series is the work of a community of people. Many contributed their time and talent to make it possible. Recognizing the work of that unseen community is to me an important confirmation that we have learned the lessons God has been teaching his people for more than three thousand years. Here are the people God has used to make this study possible.

The Prince Foundation:

The vision of Elsa and Ed Prince — that this project that began in 1993 would enable thousands of people around the world to walk in the footsteps of the people of God — has never waned. God continues to use Elsa's commitment to share God's story with our broken world.

Focus on the Family:

Jim Mhoon — vice president, content development

Mitchell Wright — executive producer, visual media

Erin Berriman — lead coordinating producer

Paul Murphy — manager, video post-production

Blain Andersen — video editor

Christi Lynn — director, product marketing

Allison Montjoy — manager, product marketing

Kay Leavy — senior coordinator, resource marketing

Larry Weeden — director, book and curriculum development and acquisition

Carol Eidson — project coordinator, business services

Zondervan:

John Raymond — vice president and publisher, curriculum

Robin Phillips — project manager, curriculum

Casper Hamlet — marketing director, curriculum

T. J. Rathbun — director, audio/visual production

Tammy Johnson — art director

Ben Fetterley, Denise Froehlich — book interior designers

Greg Clouse — production editor

That the World May Know:

Chris Hayden — research assistant. This series would not have been completed nor would it have the excellence of content it has without his outstanding research effort.

Lois Tverberg, PhD

Nadav Hillebrand

Alison Elders

Lisa Fredicks

Grooters Productions:

John Grooters — producer/director

Judy Grooters — producer

Mark Chamberlin — director of photography

Mark Chamberlin, John Grooters, Adam Vardy, Tyler Jackson — cinematography

Kent Esmeier — online editor/colorist

Alan Arroyo — assistant editor

Paul Wesselink — re-recording mixer & sound design

Christian Nikkel, Aleece Cook — additional sound

Carlos Martinez — orchestrations

Brittany Grooters, Jordyn Osburn, Hannah Dozeman, Hollie Noble — post-production assistants

Dave Lassanske, Shawn Kamerman, Eric Schrotenboer, Kate Chamberlin — camera assistants

Paul Wesselink, Ryan Wert — production sound

Dennis Lassanske, Alan Arroyo, Brittany Grooters, Taylor Wogomon, Hannah Dozeman, Nola Tolsma — production support

Taylor Wogoman, Dave Lassanske — motion graphics

Breana Melvin, Charlie Shaw, Rob Perry, John Walker, Drew Johnson — illustrators

Eric Schrotenboer — music

Sorenson Communications:

Stephen and Amanda Sorenson — writers

BIBLIOGRAPHY

Bailey, Kenneth E. *The Cross and the Prodigal: The 15th Chapter of Luke, Seen Through the Eyes of Middle Eastern Peasants*. St. Louis: Concordia, 1973.

_____. *Finding the Lost: Cultural Keys to Luke 15*. St Louis: Concordia, 1992.

_____. *Jacob and the Prodigal*. Downers Grove, Ill.: IVP Academic, 2003.

_____. *Poet and Peasant and Through Peasant Eyes*. Grand Rapids: Eerdmans, 1983.

Beitzel, Barry J. *Moody Bible Atlas*. Chicago: Moody Press, 1985.

Berlin, Adele, and Marc Zvi Brettler. *Jewish Study Bible*. Philadelphia: Jewish Publication Society and New York: Oxford University Press, 2004.

Bivin, David. *New Light on the Difficult Words of Jesus: Insights from His Jewish Context*. Holland, Mich.: EnGedi Resource Center, 2005. (www.egrc.net).

Danby, Herbert. *The Mishnah*. New York: Oxford University Press, 1977, Sanhedrin 4.5.

Fretheim, Terrence E. *Exodus: Interpretation: A Bible Commentary for Teaching and Preaching*. Louisville: John Knox Press, 1991.

Friedman, Richard Elliot. *Commentary on the Torah*. San Francisco: HarperCollins, 2001.

Hillers, Delbert R. *Covenant: The History of a Biblical Idea*. Baltimore: Johns Hopkins Press, 1969.

Hoffmeier, James K. *Ancient Israel in Sinai*. New York: Oxford University Press, 2011.

Jeremias, J. *The Parables of Jesus*. London: SCM Press, 1963.

Kline, Meredith G. *Treaty of the Great King*. Grand Rapids: William B. Eerdmans, 1962.

Levenson, Jon D. *Sinai and Zion: An Entry into the Jewish Bible*. San Francisco: HarperOne, 1987.

Levine, Baruch A. *The JPS Torah Commentary: Leviticus*. Philadelphia: Jewish Publication Society, 1991.

Milgrom, Jacob. *The JPS Torah Commentary: Numbers*. Philadelphia: Jewish Publication Society, 1991.

Notley, Steven R., and Ze'ev Safrai. *Parables of the Sages*. Jerusalem: Carta, 2011.

Pryor, Dwight A. *Unveiling the Kingdom of Heaven*. Dayton: Center for Judaic Christian Studies, 2008.

Richter, Sandra L. *The Epic of Eden*. Downers Grove, Ill.: IVP Academic, 2008.

Riskin, Shlomo. Torah Lights, Vol. 2, *Exodus Defines the Birth of a Nation*. New York: Urim Publications, 2006.

Ryken, Leland, James C. Wilhoit, and Tremper Longman III. *Dictionary of Biblical Imagery*. Downers Grove, Ill.: InterVarsity Press, 1998.

Sarna, Nahum M. *Exploring Exodus: The Origins of Biblical Israel*. New York: Schocken Books, 1996.

_____. *The JPS Torah Commentary: Exodus*. Philadelphia: Jewish Publication Society, 1991.

_____. *The JPS Torah Commentary: Genesis*. Philadelphia: Jewish Publication Society, 1991.

Telushkin, Rabbi Joseph. *The Book of Jewish Values*. New York: Bell Tower Publishers, 2000p. 70.

Tigay, Jeffrey H. The *JPS Torah Commentary: Deuteronomy*. Philadelphia: Jewish Publication Society, 1991.

Tverberg, Lois. *Walking in the Dust of Rabbi Jesus*. Grand Rapids: Zondervan, 2012.

Tverberg, Lois and Ann Spangler. *Sitting at the Feet of Rabbi Jesus*. Grand Rapids: Zondervan, 2009.

Tverberg, Lois with Bruce Okkema. *Listening to the Language of the Bible*. Holland, Mich.: En Gedi Resource Center, 2004, (www.egrc.net).

Wright, Christopher J. H. *The Mission of God*. Downers Grove, Ill.: IVP Academic, 2006.

Young, Brad H. *The Parables: Jewish Tradition and Christian Interpretation*. Peabody, Mass.: Hendrickson, 1998.

Ziony Zevit, "Three Ways to Look at the Ten Plagues," *Bible Review* (June 1990).

More Great Resources
from Focus on the Family®

Volume 1: Promised Land

This volume focuses on the Old Testament—particularly on the nation of ancient Israel, God's purpose for His people, and why He placed them in the Promised Land.

Volume 2: Prophets and Kings of Israel

This volume looks into the nation of Israel during Old Testament times to understand how the people struggled with the call of God to be a seperate and holy nation.

Volume 3: Life and Ministry of the Messiah

This volume explores the life and teaching ministry of Jesus. Discover new insights about the Son of God.

Volume 4: Death and Resurrection of the Messiah

Witness the passion of the Messiah as He resolutely sets His face toward Jerusalem to suffer and die for His bride. Discover the thrill the disciples felt when they learned of His resurrection and were later filled with the Holy Spirit.

Volume 5: Early Church

Capture the fire of the early church in this fifth set of That the World May Know® film series. See how the first Christians lived out their faith with a passion that literally changed the world.

Volume 6: In the Dust of the Rabbi

"Follow the rabbi, drink in his words, and be covered with the dust of his feet," says the ancient Jewish proverb. Come discover how to follow Jesus as you walk with teacher and historian Ray Vander Laan through the breathtaking terrains of Israel and Turkey and explore what it really means to be a disciple.

Volume 7: Walk as Jesus Walked

Journey to Israel where the 12 disciples walked the walk their rabbi Jesus taught them. Examining the culture and the politics of the first century. Ray Vander Laan opens up the Gospels as never before.

FOR MORE INFORMATION

Online:
Go to ThatTheWorldMayKnow.com

Phone:
Call toll-free: 800-A-FAMILY (232-6459)
In Canada, call toll-free: 800-661-9800

Volume 8: God Heard Their Cry

Just when it seemed that Pharaoh could not be defeated, God provided for His People in ways they never could have imagined. Join historian Ray Vander Laan in ancient Egypt for his study of God's faithfulness to the Israelites—and promise that remains true today.

Volume 9: Fire on the Mountain

When the Israelites left Egypt, they were finally free. Free from persecution, free from oppression, and free to worship their own God. But with that freedom comes a new challenge—learning how to live together the way God intends. In this ninth set of That the World May Know® film series, discover how God teaches the Israelites what it means to be part of a community that loves Him, and the lessons we can begin to live out in our lives today.

Volume 10: With All Your Heart

Do you remember where your blessings come from? In Exodus, God warned Israel to remember Him when they left the dry desert and reached the fertile fields of the promised land. But in this tenth volume of That the World May Know® film series, discover how quickly the Israelites forgot God and began to rely on themselves.

Volume 11: The Path to the Cross

Discover how the Israelites' passionate faith prepares the way for Jesus and His ultimate act of obedience and sacrifice at the cross. Then, be challenged in your own life to live as they did by every word that comes from the mouth of God.

Volume 12: Walking With God in the Desert

Are you going through a difficult period of life? The loss of a loved one? Unemployment? A crisis of faith? During these desert times, it's easy to think God has disappeared. Instead, discover that it's only when we are totally dependent on Him that we find Him closer than ever and can experience God's amazing grace and provision.